New Directions in Assessing Performance Potential of Individuals and Groups

WORKSHOP SUMMARY

Robert Pool, *Rapporteur*

Committee on Measuring Human Capabilities:
Performance Potential of Individuals and Collectives

Board on Behavioral, Cognitive, and Sensory Sciences

Division of Behavioral and Social Sciences and Education

NATIONAL RESEARCH COUNCIL
OF THE NATIONAL ACADEMIES

THE NATIONAL ACADEMIES PRESS
Washington, D.C.
www.nap.edu

THE NATIONAL ACADEMIES PRESS 500 Fifth Street, NW Washington, DC 20001

NOTICE: The project that is the subject of this report was approved by the Governing Board of the National Research Council, whose members are drawn from the councils of the National Academy of Sciences, the National Academy of Engineering, and the Institute of Medicine. The members of the committee responsible for the report were chosen for their special competences and with regard for appropriate balance.

This study was supported by Contract/Grant No. W-911NF-12-1-0504 between the National Academy of Sciences and the U.S. Department of the Army. Any opinions, findings, conclusions, or recommendations expressed in this publication are those of the author(s) and do not necessarily reflect the views of the organizations or agencies that provided support for the project.

International Standard Book Number-13: 978-0-309-29044-9
International Standard Book Number-10: 0-309-29044-9

Additional copies of this report are available from the National Academies Press, 500 Fifth Street, NW, Keck 360, Washington, DC 20001; (800) 624-6242 or (202) 334-3313; http://www.nap.edu.

Printed in the United States of America

Suggested citation: National Research Council. (2013). *New Directions in Assessing Performance Potential of Individuals and Groups: Workshop Summary.* R. Pool, Rapporteur. Committee on Measuring Human Capabilities: Performance Potential of Individuals and Collectives, Board on Behavioral, Cognitive, and Sensory Sciences. Division of Behavioral and Social Sciences and Education. Washington, DC: The National Academies Press.

THE NATIONAL ACADEMIES

Advisers to the Nation on Science, Engineering, and Medicine

The **National Academy of Sciences** is a private, nonprofit, self-perpetuating society of distinguished scholars engaged in scientific and engineering research, dedicated to the furtherance of science and technology and to their use for the general welfare. Upon the authority of the charter granted to it by the Congress in 1863, the Academy has a mandate that requires it to advise the federal government on scientific and technical matters. Dr. Ralph J. Cicerone is president of the National Academy of Sciences.

The **National Academy of Engineering** was established in 1964, under the charter of the National Academy of Sciences, as a parallel organization of outstanding engineers. It is autonomous in its administration and in the selection of its members, sharing with the National Academy of Sciences the responsibility for advising the federal government. The National Academy of Engineering also sponsors engineering programs aimed at meeting national needs, encourages education and research, and recognizes the superior achievements of engineers. Dr. C. D. Mote, Jr., is president of the National Academy of Engineering.

The **Institute of Medicine** was established in 1970 by the National Academy of Sciences to secure the services of eminent members of appropriate professions in the examination of policy matters pertaining to the health of the public. The Institute acts under the responsibility given to the National Academy of Sciences by its congressional charter to be an adviser to the federal government and, upon its own initiative, to identify issues of medical care, research, and education. Dr. Harvey V. Fineberg is president of the Institute of Medicine.

The **National Research Council** was organized by the National Academy of Sciences in 1916 to associate the broad community of science and technology with the Academy's purposes of furthering knowledge and advising the federal government. Functioning in accordance with general policies determined by the Academy, the Council has become the principal operating agency of both the National Academy of Sciences and the National Academy of Engineering in providing services to the government, the public, and the scientific and engineering communities. The Council is administered jointly by both Academies and the Institute of Medicine. Dr. Ralph J. Cicerone and Dr. C. D. Mote, Jr., are chair and vice chair, respectively, of the National Research Council.

www.national-academies.org

COMMITTEE ON MEASURING HUMAN CAPABILIITES: PERFORMANCE POTENTIAL OF INDIVIDUALS AND COLLECTIVES

Jack W. Stuster (*Chair*), Anacapa Sciences, Inc., Santa Barbara, CA
Georgia T. Chao, Eli Broad Graduate School of Management, Michigan State University
Randall W. Engle, School of Psychology, Georgia Institute of Technology
Leaetta Hough, Dunnette Group, Ltd., Saint Paul, MN
Patrick C. Kyllonen, Center for Academic and Workforce Readiness and Success, Educational Testing Service, Princeton, NJ
John J. McArdle, Department of Psychology, University of Southern California
Stephen Stark, Department of Psychology, University of South Florida

Cherie Chauvin, *Study Director*
Tina Winters, *Associate Program Officer*
Renée L. Wilson Gaines, *Senior Program Assistant*

Acknowledgments

This workshop summary is based on the proceedings of a public workshop held on April 3-4, 2013, convened by the Board on Behavioral, Cognitive, and Sensory Sciences, and planned by the Committee on Measuring Human Capabilities: Performance Potential of Individuals and Collectives. The planning committee members identified research areas of interest and specific presenters, organized the agenda, and facilitated roundtable discussions; however, they did not participate in the writing of this summary. Its contents reflect their diligent planning efforts, the insightful presentations of invited experts, and the thought-provoking roundtable discussions of all invited participants as well as the general audience.

The workshop, and the larger study for which it is a part, was sponsored by the U.S. Army Research Institute for the Behavioral and Social Sciences (ARI). In particular, the committee wishes to thank Gerald Goodwin, chief of foundational science at ARI, and his entire research team, for their support and guidance throughout the planning process.

Among the National Research Council (NRC) staff, special thanks are due to Barbara A. Wanchisen who provided oversight to the process of planning and hosting the workshop. Additionally, special thanks to Tina Winters, associate program officer, who was in many ways the life of this workshop. She dedicated countless hours to organizing this large public event, including working extensively with each presenter and panelist to refine their planned remarks in light of the event's goals and the planning committee's intentions. Renée L. Wilson Gaines, senior program assistant, also provided critical logistical and administrative support to the event, including coordinating the details of the event's special location. We also thank NRC consultants Robert Pool for his assistance in drafting the summary and Robert Katt for final editing of the manuscript. And finally we thank the executive office reports staff of the Division of Behavioral and Social Sciences and Education, especially Kirsten Sampson Snyder, who managed the review process, and Yvonne Wise, who oversaw the final publication process.

This summary has been reviewed in draft form by individuals chosen for their diverse perspectives and technical expertise, in accordance with procedures approved by the NRC's Report Review Committee. The purpose of this independent review is to provide candid and critical comments that will assist the institution in making its published summary as sound as possible and to ensure that the summary meets institutional standards for objectivity, evidence, and responsiveness to the study charge. The review comments and draft manuscript remain confidential to protect the integrity of the deliberative process. We wish to thank the following individuals for their review of this summary: Jennifer S. Cole, Department of Linguistics, University of Illinois at Urbana-Champaign; Neal W. Schmitt, Department of Psychology and Management, Michigan State University; Robert Sternberg, Department of Psychology, Yale University; William J. Strickland, president and chief executive officer, Human Resources Research Organization, Alexandria, Virginia; and Mary D. Zalesny, office of the Chief of Staff of the Army Strategic Studies Group, Arlington, Virginia.

Although the reviewers listed above provided many constructive comments and suggestions, they were not asked to endorse the content of the report nor did they see the final draft of the report before its release. The review of this report was overseen by Nancy T. Tippins, senior vice president and managing principal, Valtera Corporation. Appointed by the NRC, she was responsible for making certain that an independent examination of this summary was carried out in accordance with institutional procedures and that all review comments were carefully considered. Responsibility for the final content of this summary rests entirely with the rapporteur and the institution.

Contents

1

Introduction

As an all-volunteer service accepting applications from nearly 400,000 potential recruits annually from across the U.S. population, the U.S. military must accurately and efficiently assess the individual capability of each recruit for the purposes of selection, job classification, and unit assignment. In light of this continual challenge, the U.S. Army Research Institute for the Behavioral and Social Sciences (ARI) requested that the National Research Council (NRC) conduct a study to examine the future of military entrance assessments. On April 3-4, 2013, the committee appointed by the NRC to conduct this study, the Committee on Measuring Human Capabilities: Performance Potential of Individuals and Collectives, held a workshop on the topic of "New Directions in Assessing Individuals and Groups."

In advance of the workshop, participants were invited to read materials provided by ARI to familiarize them with current Army selection practices. The opening pages of the 2011 ARI special report, *Select for Success*, capture the spirit in which this workshop was planned and hosted:

> What if the Army could
>
> … screen out low motivated, low performing applicants?
> … screen in highly motivated, high performing applicants?
> … better predict APFT [army physical fitness test] success?
> … reduce the number of Soldiers who attrit before commitment completion?

> … reduce the time and effort units devote to dealing with problem Soldiers?
> … select Soldiers who are more satisfied with the Army and their MOS [military occupation specialty]?
> … select Soldiers who are more likely to espouse and reflect Army values? (U.S. Army Research Institute for the Behavioral and Social Sciences, 2011, p. 1)

For these reasons and others, it is increasingly important that the U.S. Army leverage effective means to select and assign personnel. To that end, this study in its entirety was designed to investigate cutting-edge research into the measurement of both individual capabilities and group composition in order to identify future research directions that may lead to improved assessment and selection of enlisted personnel for the U.S. Army. The first phase of the study included a workshop to which scientists from a variety of relevant areas were invited to discuss research that bears on the issues at hand. (The statement of task for the study's first phase is reproduced in Box 1-1.) In the second phase, the committee will consider in more depth the research areas discussed at the workshop, as well as additional areas of research, and will develop consensus conclusions and recommendations to inform future research related to the measurement of individual and group capabilities. The ultimate goal of both the workshop and the committee report is to inform the design of a maximally effective selection and assessment system.

As committee chair Jack Stuster of Anacapa Sciences, Inc., noted in his introductory comments, the goal of the workshop was "to encourage interdisciplinary dialogue on the current and future state-of-the-science in measurement of individual capability and the combination of individual capabilities to create collective capacity to perform." The workshop emphasized cognitive and noncognitive attributes that can be used in the initial testing and assignment of enlisted personnel. Certain topics were excluded from consideration, including physical attributes and skills, endocrinology or blood chemistry indicators of performance, genetic screening, biographical data as predictors of performance, birth-order effects, work samples, miniature training and evaluation technologies, and mid-career and post-injury assessments. Some of these were excluded because of ethical considerations, while others were excluded because of the practical needs of standardized and mass testing.

The specific workshop topics included

- the evolving goals of candidate testing,
- emerging constructs and theory,
- ethical implications of testing methods,

BOX 1-1
Phase 1 Statement of Task

An ad hoc committee will plan and host a public workshop to encourage interdisciplinary dialogue on the current and future state-of-the-science in measurement of individual capability and the combination of individual capabilities to create collective capacity to perform. The workshop will feature invited presentations and discussions to address the following questions:

1. Beyond tests of cognitive ability (e.g., Armed Services Vocational Aptitude Battery [ASVAB]) and personality (e.g., Tailored Adaptive Personality Assessment System [TAPAS]) already in use by the U.S. Army, which cutting-edge areas of research, including those already being investigated by the U.S. Army Research Institute (ARI), may provide new and unique scientifically valid methods for measuring individual capabilities and predicting individual and collective performance?
2. Are there recent or emerging theoretical, technological, and/or statistical advances that have enabled new approaches and/or measurement capabilities with respect to the measurement of individual capability and the combination of individual capabilities to create collective capacity to perform?
3. Are there neuroscience or psychophysiology advances related specifically to the understanding of individual differences that suggest new ways to approach empirical research and theory development in this area? If so, what are they, who are the researchers, and how might they be applied in ARI's basic research program?
4. ARI would benefit from an interdisciplinary discussion of "gaps" and potential research related specifically to theories of individual differences (cognitive, affective, personality, social or interpersonal skills), testing and measurement methods, test theory, statistical and mathematical modeling of collective/group/team performance, and the combination of individual capabilities to create collective capacity to perform. Which "gaps" exist in the scientific findings? Which "gaps" appear the most promising for future research with potential near-term payoff?

The discussion and major themes that emerge from the workshop will be synthesized in an individually authored workshop summary.

- measuring individual differences and predicting individual performance,
- group composition processes and performance, and
- crosscutting links and research gaps.

By bringing together scientists from a variety of areas of research, the workshop was designed to explore interdisciplinary scientific approaches to individual and group assessments and to identify promising concepts for further consideration. The overall study is designed to inform the development of near-term basic research programs leading to applied research and specific applications in the long term. Therefore, many of the discussions were more broadly applicable to a wide range of testing and assessment conditions, rather than to the narrowly focused needs of Army assessment and selection.

This publication is a summary and synthesis of the two-day workshop held in fulfillment of phase 1 of the study. Readers of this summary should keep in mind that it is only reporting on the presentations and discussions of individuals at the workshop. In particular, any opinions, conclusions, or recommendations reported here are solely those of the individuals who offered them. The presentations and discussions were limited by the time available for the workshop; see the Appendix for the workshop agenda and list of participants. Potentially important subjects and areas of research that were not covered during the workshop are not included here, and their omission from this summary should not be interpreted as an assessment of their value, but only that time did not allow their inclusion. There was no attempt to reach consensus at the workshop, and any statements that appear in this workshop summary should not be taken as indicative of the ultimate conclusions and recommendations that the committee may include in its final report at the end of the second phase. This summary was prepared by a rapporteur and summarizes views expressed by individual workshop participants. The NRC is responsible only for its overall quality and accuracy as a record of what transpired at the workshop.

REFERENCE

U.S. Army Research Institute for the Behavioral and Social Sciences. (2011). *Select for Success: A Toolset for Enhancing Soldier Accessioning*. Special Report 70. Available: http://www.dtic.mil/cgi-bin/GetTRD?AD=ADA554057 [July 2013].

2

Overview

As long as there have been armies, there has been a need to assess soldiers' capabilities and predict their likely performance. Speaking of the Army of Ephesus 2,500 years ago, Heraclitus observed:

> Out of every 100 men, 10 shouldn't even be there, 80 are just targets. Nine are the real fighters, and we are lucky to have them, for they make the battle. Ah, but the one. One is a warrior and he will bring the others back.

Jack Stuster, chair of the Committee on Measuring Human Capabilities, noted in his introductory comments to the workshop that, for thousands of years, one of the keys to successfully assembling an army is to select the right soldiers—to accurately predict which individuals are likely to succeed and which are likely to fail. "In the modern era," Stuster also said, "you have probably heard the adage that amateurs talk about tactics, while professionals talk about logistics. Well, [the military writer] Tom Ricks wrote recently that real insiders talk about personnel policy, because they know it provides the foundation for everything in the military."

To set the stage for the workshop, the initial presentations provided invited participants and audience members with the past, present, and future context of military assessment and assessment science. Following Stuster's opening remarks, Gerald Goodwin, representing the U.S. Army Research Institute for the Behavioral and Social Sciences (ARI), the study sponsor, provided his perspective on the purpose and need for this workshop as well as the larger study, to include the committee's final report.

To provide an overview of the variety of research that the military may be able to use in improving its assessments, Fred Oswald spoke on the present and future of assessment science.

THE CONTEXT OF MILITARY ASSESSMENT

In providing the study sponsor's perspective, Gerald Goodwin, chief of foundational science at ARI, offered context for the discussions to come with a brief description of the U.S. Army's current assessments and anticipated directions for the future. The current assessments used by the Army, he noted, have their roots in classical test theory, which was developed in the early 1900s [though not published until much later, see Novick, 1966]. From there, measurement theory slowly evolved until the current standard, item response theory (IRT), was developed in the 1950s and 1960s. Minor variants and additions have emerged along the way, such as generalizability theory, which was used for parsing measurement variance beyond "true" score and error. But on the whole, Goodwin noted, IRT is today's dominant theory for cutting-edge psychological assessments.

"Given that item response theory first came onto the scene in the late 1950s, which is 50-plus years ago," Goodwin observed, "What I am interested in is, what is next? What is the next wave that is going to drive psychological assessment for the next 50 years? Where is that coming from, and how do we start to codify that, so that we are moving in the direction of developing that theory and getting it to a robust state, so that we can all be using it for psychological assessments over the next 50 years?"

Today, the Army's base assessment tool for cognitive assessment and vocational skills is the Armed Services Vocational Aptitude Battery, or ASVAB. It was originally developed in the 1970s, and in the 1990s it was updated for computerized adaptive testing as CAT-ASVAB (see Sands et al., 1999). Currently, the test includes nine sections of multiple-choice questions covering general science, arithmetic reasoning, mathematics knowledge, word knowledge, paragraph comprehension, electronics information, automotive and shop information, mechanical comprehension, and object assembling.[1] The pool of questions from which the test draws is renewed every couple of years.

In addition, Goodwin said, the military services recently began supplementing the ASVAB with personality assessments. The Army developed, in collaboration with Drasgow Consulting Group, the Tailored Adaptive Personality Assessment System (TAPAS), which assesses many of the facets of the Big Five personality traits (openness, conscientious-

[1]See http://www.official-asvab.com/whattoexpect_rec.htm [July 2013] for the most up-to-date information on the content of the ASVAB.

ness, extraversion, agreeableness, and emotional stability; see Digman, 1990; Tupes, 1957; Tupes and Christal, 1961) and several of the subfacets, as well as a few personality measures that are specific to the Army. "That is really at a cutting-edge stage in terms of personnel assessment right now," he said.

In explaining the rationale for requesting this study, Goodwin noted that one of ARI's missions is to be "the developer of the science underlying the personnel assessment and testing program for the Army." Goodwin explained that he reviewed ARI's basic research program (for which he is responsible), as well as its applied program, in personnel assessment, and considered the dominant theories and measurements in use over the past 50 years or so. He then asked, "Given where we are, and the state of personnel testing in the military, can the committee provide recommendations for basic research in terms of scientific investment [to address the questions described in the following section]?" The workshop was thus intended and planned as the primary data gathering opportunity on potential advances and areas of research the committee may subsequently consider in recommending future investments by ARI's basic research program.

Potential Future Directions

Having provided an overview of the past and present context of military assessments, Goodwin then described how he imagines assessments of the future. He outlined his vision through several questions concerning basic scientific research, which he identified for discussion during the workshop and which the committee has been asked to address in its final report (at the completion of the study's second phase).

New Constructs

First, because new constructs and concepts may allow the Army to develop better measures of performance, Goodwin asked, "What are new constructs that we should be measuring, and how do we think about constructs in potentially a different way?" From Goodwin's perspective, it is important that the search is not limited to simply looking broadly in the psychological literature for more constructs and for different constructs. Instead, he is interested in stepping back and asking whether it would be valuable to think about individual differences in a different format, in order to identify new constructs not previously considered.

The reason for the Army's interest, he said, is that there is a lot of work going on now in the areas of psychophysiology and neuroscience that "speak to individual differences in a different format and in a different language than how we talk about them in psychological science." Can that work be used, he asked, to improve the current understanding of individual differences and to provide new avenues for improving the prediction of performance?

New Measurement Methods and Theory

Goodwin also explained that, simultaneously with the exploration of new constructs, the Army is looking for ways to improve its measurement of various factors.[2] To consider the theories necessary as foundations for potential improvements, Goodwin asked, "What are the advances in psychometric theory that can help us get past some of the hurdles and the boundary conditions that exist in psychometric theory now?" As an example, he noted that both classical test theory and item response theory work best when each item measures only one construct. But what happens, he asked, when a single item measures more than one construct? "How do we . . . assign scores for the individual constructs when we have one item that is measuring multiple things? How do we create a test that would work with that?"

A second way to improve measurement, according to Goodwin, is to develop new measurement methods. There are already a large number of different types of measurement methods, with new methods in development all the time. What else is out there that could help the Army develop better assessments? In particular, he asked, "What are the cutting-edge ideas that exist in the small pockets of science out there that haven't hit the mainstream yet? We are looking for the good ideas, as places that we might be able to take personnel assessment in the future." Of particular interest are "unobtrusive" methods of measurement—methods that measure behaviors or constructs while the individual is engaged in a complex task, without interfering in that task.

Future Applications

Finally, Goodwin explained that the Army is interested in moving beyond assessment for selection into the military and into assessment for a particular team or unit. "Right now," Goodwin said, "we predict individual performance and individual potential fairly well" with respect to selecting recruits into the military and to assigning occupational job cat-

[2]Various presenters and participants at the workshop used the terms "construct," "factor," and "trait" in ways that appear to make them near-synonyms. This summary has kept the terminology used by a particular speaker, but readers should bear in mind that these terms may be used interchangeably.

egories. But the next step—assignment into a particular unit—will require additional thought on exactly what needs to be predicted.

Is the goal to predict individual performance in a unit? It is not that simple, Goodwin observed, because individual performance in a unit depends on a number of other factors, including characteristics of other team members. Thus it is possible that the goal may be to predict group performance or unit performance. If so, he said, "How do we start from individual level scores and individual constructs to get to unit performance, and how do we better understand that process?" There is some research being done in the area now, but it is not yet mainstream. Thus, he asked, "What are the good ideas in this area that we [ARI] might be able to invest in, that might turn into a reality 15 to 20 years down the line?"

Boundary Conditions

Ultimately, Goodwin cautioned, the adoption of any new assessment methods by the Army will require satisfaction of certain boundary conditions. First, testing methods must be mass administrable. The Army tests huge numbers of people—up to 400,000 each year—to bring about 200,000 into active service. "This is not something that we can do in a cost-inefficient way," he said. "The Department of Defense . . . simply can't afford it."

Additionally, the tests must be administrable in an unproctored format or by personnel not skilled in highly technical test administration, such as military recruiters. "We can't have tests that must be administered by folks who have advanced degrees in psychometrics or advanced degrees in neuroscience." That leaves out such highly technical possibilities as using magnetic resonance imagery (MRI) exams as part of the assessment, he noted.

Furthermore, most if not all of the tests must be done in "pre-accessioning," which is the period before a recruit joins the Army. "Again, this is a cost investment piece," he explained. The cost to replace an individual who drops out of basic training is about $73,000 per person. "Using basic training as a selection venue isn't workable because that is a huge cost investment."

ARI, as a part of the scientific community, is tackling the challenge of assessment from a scientific perspective. Constructs considered for research and ultimately for application must be based upon fundamentally good scientific theory. "Understanding how the theory works—and how it works in concert with all of the other psychological theory out there—is critical to us," Goodwin emphasized.

The final boundary condition Goodwin discussed is that any changes to the current assessment program should have the promise of maintaining, if not increasing, testing efficiency—that is, providing as much or more measurement in the same or less amount of time and with the same or greater predictive value. New methods should maintain or improve the cost–benefit balance. If the tests are more expensive, they will need to provide extra benefits that justify the added cost. Goodwin underscored the point that the Army will not, and cannot, pay more for the same or less value.

THE PRESENT AND FUTURE OF ASSESSMENT SCIENCE

After Goodwin provided the past, present, and future context of military assessment, Fred Oswald, a professor of industrial and organizational psychology at Rice University in Houston, Texas, provided an overview of the current state and likely future directions of the science of assessment, with an eye toward areas that might be of particular interest to the military.

Domains of Performance

There are countless determinants of performance that are relevant to success in one's job, Oswald noted. Furthermore, there are key determinants of performance that are indicated by different malleable and nonmalleable skills; declarative and procedural knowledge; technical, social, physical and psychomotor skills; and motivation that guides the direction, intensity, and frequency of performance. To provide a general picture of the many different aspects of performance, Oswald offered a list of broad domains of performance with a few examples of criteria for each nonphysical domain:

- Foundational behaviors
    - Performs routine duties
    - Communicates effectively
- Technical/intellectual behaviors
    - Produces training or work products
    - Solves individual and team problems
- Leadership behaviors
    - Seeks internal and/or external strategic information
    - Delegates, sets goals, and motivates others
    - Develops work climate
- Intrapersonal behaviors
    - Demonstrates initiative
    - Perseveres under pressure
    - Shows commitment (versus counterproductive work behavior)

    - Handles work stress (versus withdrawal/attrition)
    - Follows rules/procedures
- Interpersonal behaviors
    - Helps others voluntarily
    - Provides emotional support
    - Offers technical support
    - Acts flexibly with teammates
- Physical behaviors

"You will see that the span of criteria and complexity is vast," he said. "It spans technical and nontechnical domains. It spans across individuals and groups, . . . and there is a time dimension that goes through all of this, to make things even more complex."

Given this vast range, Oswald observed, it is a difficult and complex problem to determine which types of performance are important in any given setting. "Not all of these criteria are important for any particular setting," Oswald explained, "but I suspect that more than one criterion is important for [a] particular situation, and therefore [one is] faced with a multivariate case, and complexity begins as soon as you start talking about that." Oswald believes the development of new criteria will only make this problem more challenging.

Determinants of Performance

To predict the likely performance of an individual or a group, Oswald noted, it is necessary to measure performance or various determinants of performance, such as knowledge, skills, or motivation. Some types of performance are malleable and may improve or decline over time, he observed, while others remain constant; the same is true for determinants of performance. Which types are malleable and which are not, according to Oswald, is something that generally should be tested empirically.

Any reliable performance measure of interest to the Army, according to Oswald, should be a function of declarative knowledge, procedural knowledge, motivation, or a combination of these three determinants. Declarative knowledge includes knowing facts, rules, and strategies—all things that can generally be tested with direct questioning. Procedural knowledge can be demonstrated in one way or another, though not necessarily questioned directly. The knowledge does not have to be explicit, Oswald noted. There are various sorts of implicit procedural knowledge, such as skill in driving a car with a stick shift, which has some psychomotor aspects to it.

Motivation, the third performance determinant, is the willingness and ability to apply the knowledge possessed. "Whether one is willing to perform," Oswald explained, "depends on a number of different intrinsic and extrinsic factors that guide direction and choice, how intensely you perform, and how often you perform."

Traditional Measurement

Next, Oswald turned toward the question of how to carry out complex measurements "where we are trying to pack many constructs in, in a short amount of time." He discussed two different approaches that are typically applied, one that is more traditional and one that is more modern. In his discussion of integrating these practical approaches, he offered a brief factor analysis of each construct to be measured.

One way to carry out measurements on a number of constructs simultaneously, he said, is to examine a construct that is hierarchical in nature. One example of such a construct is core self-evaluation (CSE; defined as an individual's appraisal of their self-worth and capabilities; see Chang et al., 2012, for a review), which is composed of four different personality traits: (1) self-esteem, (2) generalized self-efficacy, (3) emotional stability, and (4) locus of control (see Figure 2-1).

There are various approaches to measuring CSE. One could, for example, conduct a factor analysis on all the items used to measure the four individual constructs and extract the general factor; this general factor approach would result in a collection of items that are related to one another yet are sampled from across the four traits that contribute to the composite construct of CSE. However, with this approach, there is no guarantee that the items selected will represent each of the constituent traits evenly.

A second general factor approach, which Oswald described as a controlled heterogeneity approach, would sample deliberately from each of the four traits by conducting a factor analysis within each construct, identifying the items with the highest loadings within each of them, and then combining them into a single CSE scale. Oswald explained that CSE provides a general factor that predicts a wide variety of behavior or performance outcomes, such as task performance, contextual performance, and job satisfaction. This is a very practical strategy that can serve a wide array of purposes.

An alternative to a general factor approach, Oswald noted, could be used in the case that one particular outcome—job satisfaction, for example—was of great interest. Then one could focus solely on the particular trait or traits underlying CSE that are theoretically and empirically predictive—emotional stability, for example. This *specific predictor approach* makes it possible to look at a single relationship between predictor and criterion in a very refined way and perhaps then to build up to a broader

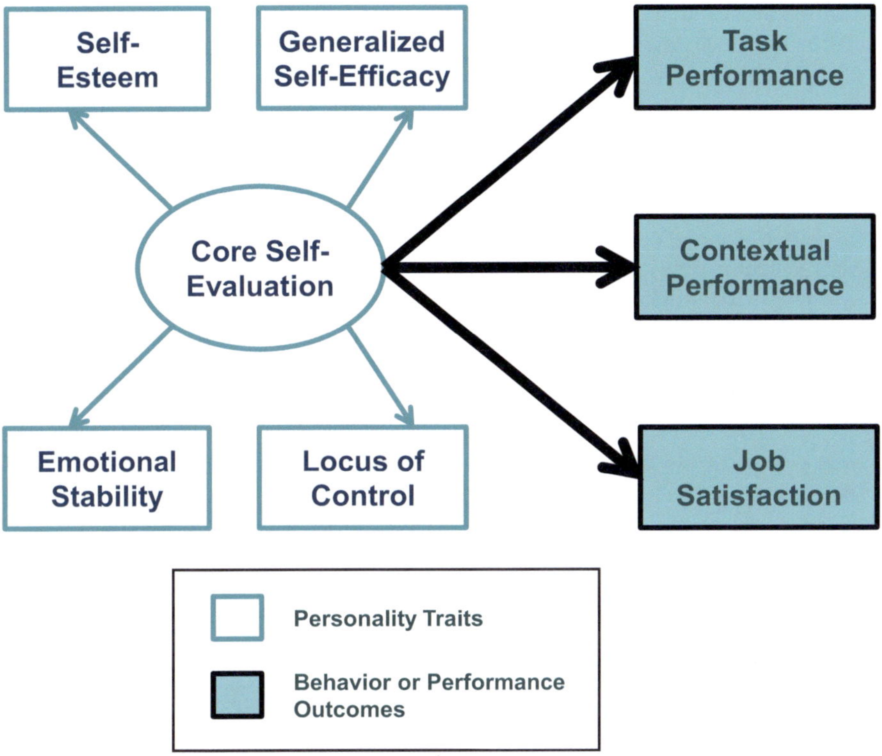

FIGURE 2-1 Measurement approach for a traditional construct: core self-evaluation.
SOURCE: Oswald presentation.

look at the network of important relationships that emerge from this bottom-up approach.

A fourth approach begins with a top-down exploratory analysis, in which one seeks to determine which relationships are important, before deciding whether to use a general factor or a specific predictor analysis. To explore the possibilities, one would look for relationships between each of the four traits ((1) self-esteem, (2) generalized self-efficacy, (3) emotional stability, and (4) locus of control) and each of the three criteria (task performance, contextual performance, and job satisfaction). Then, based on the pattern of predictions, one could decide which approach, general factor or specific predictor, might be most useful. The decision will also depend on various practical constraints, such as the amount of time available to develop or administer the measures, Oswald noted.

Moving beyond this specific example, Oswald pointed out that similar measurement approaches are applicable to any domain represented by a hierarchical structure. For example, when considering general cognitive ability (g), one deals with such contributing traits as math, spatial, and verbal abilities and may want to predict such criteria as overall job performance or effective communication skills. One is again confronted with the question of whether to use a general factor or specific predictor approach. If the objective was to predict an individual's ability to create statistical models, for instance, should one use math ability as a specific predictor or should one use an overall composite of the three traits because verbal expression may be essential to communicate the results from the models?

A similar situation arises in the personality domain, he noted, with respect to facets of personality as the factors for analysis. As an example, Oswald discussed conscientiousness as the broad general construct, with achievement striving, cautiousness, and orderliness as the facets contributing to that construct. Team-motivating behaviors, safety behaviors, and overall job performance are performance criteria that might be predicted by conscientiousness and these three personality facets.

Referring to the assessment of reliability for hierarchical traits, Oswald explained, "I call this 'traditional measurement' in quotes because we already have psychometric strategies to look at composite reliability. Classical test theory can apply here fairly readily, and this [factor analysis for hierarchical structures] has been addressed in the literature for decades."

Future Measurement

Moving on, Oswald contrasted the traditional measurement approaches with future measurement approaches that might be required to reliably measure and study complex constructs like multitasking. Oswald noted that there are many definitions of multitasking, but they all involve the ability to shift attention effectively. Regardless of its definition, he said, the construct of multitasking is clearly complex. He asked, "How might we go about predicting it? It might require measures and technologies that go beyond classical test theory types of psychometric approaches and traditional approaches to measure development itself."

As a partial answer to that question, Oswald described some of his own multitasking research. The criterion was a computer monitoring task in which the subject had to simultaneously monitor four quadrants on the computer screen (as illustrated in Figure 2-2). Each quadrant required the subject to simultaneously engage in a memory search (upper left quadrant), arithmetic (upper right quadrant), visual monitoring (lower left quadrant), and auditory monitoring tasks (lower right quadrant). Oswald's goal was to understand what individual differences might underlie differences in performance on this task.

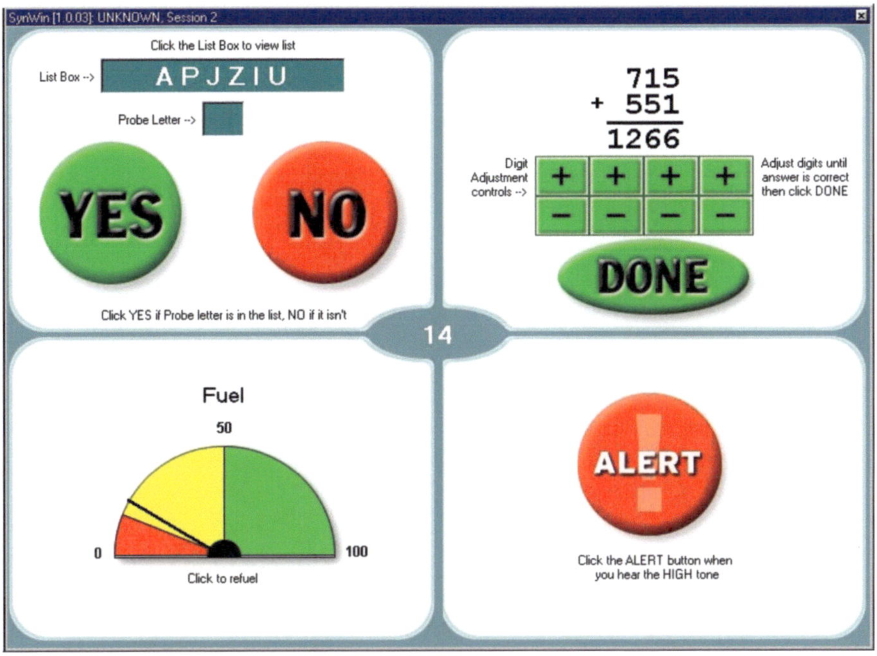

FIGURE 2-2 Example of an approach for measurement of multitasking.
SOURCE: Oswald et al. (2007, p. 7).

In Oswald's research results (see Table 2-1), general cognitive ability was the strongest predictor of multitasking performance, he noted, but it was not the only important predictor. Various other personality traits also predicted performance, but the strength of the correlation—and sometimes the direction—varied depending on the pace of the multitasking task: whether it was presented at a normal pace (see row labeled Baseline in Table 2-1) at which it was possible to accomplish all the tasks presented or at an extremely fast pace (see row labeled Emergency in Table 2-1), at which it was virtually impossible to complete all of the tasks.

Oswald added that at a normal pace, emotional stability was a strong predictor, such that "being calm and figuring out what was going on added incremental validity above ability." In the fast-paced condition, "everybody was a little bit anxious, and therefore emotional stability was less of a predictor as a trait." By contrast, conscientiousness had no correlation with performance in the normal-pace condition and had a negative relationship with task accomplishment in the fast-paced condition, presumably because greater attention to detail would make it harder to speed up performance to keep pace with the task.

TABLE 2-1 Correlations of Predictor Variables with Baseline Performance Versus Emergency Performance

Performance Block	g	ES	E	O	A	C
Baseline	**.25**	**.21**	.01	.13	.01	.00
Emergency	**.36**	.03	.02	**.17**	–.08	**–.24**

NOTES: A = agreeableness; C = conscientiousness; E = extraversion; ES = emotional stability; g = general cognitive ability; O = openness. Table values in boldface indicate statistical significance at $p < 0.05$.
SOURCE: Adapted from Oswald et al. (2007, p. 15).

The point of the example, Oswald said, was to show how these patterns of differential prediction can serve as ways of understanding the nature of a complex construct. "You might do this sort of pilot work before venturing further into a complex domain," Oswald suggested.

Classical Versus Modern Psychometrics

Generally speaking, Oswald said, classical psychometrics tends to focus on "purer" constructs, unconditional reliability, and full-scale tests. By contrast, modern psychometrics tends to focus on complex constructs and conditional reliability, in which the reliability may be dependent upon a person's trait level or upon where a subject is in the course of taking a test. "Conditional reliability gets modified over time," he noted. Furthermore, instead of full-scale tests, part of the practice of modern psychometrics focuses on ipsative or partially ipsative scales, where a subject is given a forced choice—Do you prefer X or Y?—rather than rating both X and Y on a scale. Oswald believes this opens up new methods to potentially produce better estimations. Furthermore, modern psychometrics also makes use of adaptive tests, in which the test questions change in response to previous answers, often in order to tailor the test to, for example, the subject's ability level.

In considering modern psychometric tests, Oswald said, it is important to keep in mind the principle of parsimony. "We can be lured by complex models, but from a scientific point of view, . . . complex models have to justify their departure from simpler models," he warned. Echoing Gerald Goodwin's earlier observations, Oswald emphasized that, if it is more expensive to use the more complex tests and technologies of modern psychometrics, then one should expect there to be a valuable payoff. This payoff could take the form of increased validity, but it could also come in the form of improved reliability, tests that are easier to adapt, better item security, improved ability to analyze subgroup differences, and so on.

Predictor Complexity

For Oswald, one of the more important differences between classical and modern psychometrics is in the level of predictor complexity. In classical psychometrics, the constructs—things like working memory, self-efficacy, interests, and personality factors—are purer and more determinant-like. That is, they correlate closely to one or more of the determinants of performance: declarative knowledge, procedural knowledge, or motivation.

By contrast, the complex measures of modern psychometrics involve amalgams of constructs. They are intended for such tasks as assessment of performance during multitasking activities and complex simulations, evaluation of work samples, and analysis of biodata. According to Oswald, it can be much harder to align them with the determinants of performance. Instead, they are more criterion-like, which makes it easier to apply them as measures relevant to various criteria. That can be a benefit in terms of providing greater validity, Oswald said.

The Big Picture

Continuing on, Oswald cautioned workshop participants that it is important to keep in mind that, whether the psychometrics being used are traditional or modern, the statistical concepts and practices underlying test development focus on just a small part of the broader context that is involved in understanding and predicting performance. To point out some of the things that are often missed, Oswald spoke briefly about what he called "the big picture."

For example, validity studies are generally static: "You develop a new measure, you see whether it predicts a criterion down the road," but often the data are all from one point in time. "I understand the constraints on a validity study firsthand," Oswald said. "That may be all the data you have. But there is a bigger picture, whether you have the data to research it or not, and that is that dynamics are at play. Performance does change over time." To the extent that it is possible to get data over time, such data can be quite valuable—not just of scientific value but also of practical value, as they allow an examination of changes in performance, commitment, attrition, and other criteria over time.

In addition, selection research typically reports validity coefficients that reflect direct effects between predictors and criteria—between working memory and job performance, for instance, or between interests and attrition. But there are a variety of mediators and moderators that lie between the predictors and the criteria and that play a role in explaining their relationships. Key explanatory variables include such things as organizational culture, management and leadership, team dynamics, situational stability, intrinsic and extrinsic rewards, and training knowledge. "It is not a black box," Oswald said. "It might be a black box in the sense that you might not [in a single study] be able to have all of these things [variables] for everybody at all points in time, but you might have enough people, at some points in time, to examine a mediating effect and get at this critical question [for selection] of whether the direct effect is really where all the prediction lies, or is the validity there because of the explanatory mediating effect?"

Finally, selection and classification—the focus of psychometric efforts—are part of a much larger organizational and even societal picture. Formal education and recruitment are part of a funnel that brings individuals into the Army, where they are subject to selection and classification and then to training and mentoring, which ultimately leads to individual and group performance. Then, based on performance, there is promotion, transfer, and transition. "Because selection is a critical part of this chain, selection is affected by this broader picture, and it affects the broader picture as well," Oswald said. Therefore, he concluded, investment in an expanded and integrated systems approach to personnel selection and classification could provide great value.

DISCUSSION

In the discussion that followed, committee member Randall Engle expressed the opinion that essentially all of the constructs that Oswald spoke about—self-efficacy, working memory, and so on—are more or less poorly understood in some ways. He asked Oswald whether some subconstructs might be more important than others. Are there constructs that might either supplement or supplant the current ones in terms of their importance? It would seem that these sorts of things are important to understand, he said, and that it would be useful to have some sort of process for developing new and better understanding of the constructs.

Oswald agreed. "One danger of complex measurement is that you potentially obtain validity without that understanding," he said. "By having a high validity, you can get stuck at the level of technology [the finding] and not the theory that is driving it." He added that one benefit of understanding constructs better is that it helps one develop complex measures better.

Patrick Kyllonen, also a member of the committee, commented that Oswald had spoken a great deal about the relationships between constructs. He asked whether there might be cases where the measurement itself is as important as, if not more important than, the construct it is measuring. "For example," he said, "we all might agree that conscientiousness as a construct is extremely important for success everywhere—

in education, the workforce. Yet, the way we measure conscientiousness primarily is with these rating scales. . . . We are putting a lot of weight for a very important construct on this very simplistic measurement technique." He asked what might be the expected "bang for the buck" in going after measurement methods, as opposed to figuring out such things as the relative weight of conscientiousness versus CSE.

Both avenues are important, Oswald replied, and he agreed with Kyllonen that it is important to pay attention to new and better measures.

Committee member Leaetta Hough added that while she agreed that it is important to address the measurement issue, she thought it would be premature to ignore constructs. "It wasn't so long ago that we did not have conscientiousness or hard work as part of our performance models," she said. "There may very well be other constructs out there that are important, too."

Oswald responded that the two issues, measurement and constructs, are complementary. "The more we think about measurement, the more we have fidelity to the construct of interest. We need to have a deep conceptual understanding of our construct before we can go out substantiating it in one way or another."

REFERENCES

Chang, C., D.L. Ferris, R.E. Johnson, C.C. Rosen, and J.A. Tan. (2012). Core self-evaluations: A review and evaluation of the literature. *Journal of Management,* 38(1):81-128.

Digman, J.M. (1990). Personality structure: Emergence of the five-factor model. *Annual Review of Psychology,* 41(1):417-440.

Novick, M.R. (1966). The axioms and principal results of classical test theory. *Journal of Mathematical Psychology,* 3(1):1-18.

Oswald, F.L., D.Z. Hambrick, L.A. Jones, and S.S. Ghumman. (2007). *SYRUS: Understanding and Predicting Multitasking Performance* (NPRST-TN-07-5). Millington, TN: Navy Personnel Research, Studies, and Technology.

Sands, W.A., B.K. Waters, and J.R. McBride. (1999). *CATBOOK Computerized Adaptive Testing: From Inquiry to Operation* (Study Note 99-02). Alexandria, VA: U.S. Army Research Institute for the Behavioral and Social Sciences.

Tupes, E.C. (1957). *Personality Traits Related to Effectiveness of Junior and Senior Air Force Officers* (USAF Personal Training Research, No. 57-125). Lackland Air Force Base, TX: Aeronautical Systems Division, Personnel Laboratory.

Tupes, E.C., and R.E. Christal. (1961). *Recurrent Personality Factors Based on Trait Ratings* (ASD-TR-61-97). Lackland Air Force Base, TX: Aeronautical Systems Division, Personnel Laboratory.

3

New Constructs for Assessing Individuals

Recent psychological research points toward a variety of constructs that can be used in assessments to provide greater accuracy or additional valuable information about the individuals being assessed. The workshop presenters described a number of such cutting-edge constructs, primarily during the first panel: Emerging Constructs and Theory. In this chapter, invited presentations during the first panel from Christopher Patrick, Michael Kane, and Todd Little are described, as well as the related presentation by James Rounds on interests, during the workshop's second day.

NEUROBEHAVIORAL CONSTRUCTS

Christopher Patrick, a professor of clinical psychology at Florida State University, discussed one approach to revising existing constructs and developing new constructs: the psychoneurometric approach. He defined psychoneurometrics as "the systematic development of neurobiologically based measures of individual difference constructs, using psychometric operationalizations as referents." In essence, it is a way of developing measures of individual differences by combining information and insights from neurobiology (the study of the biological aspects of the brain and nervous system) with what has been learned from psychological studies of individual differences. An associated aim of the psychoneurometric approach, Patrick continued, is to refine the individual difference constructs themselves through the incorporation of physiological data—such things as brain activity, the levels of hormones and other biological molecules, and measurements of various reflexes. "I want to work back and forth between the physiological data and the starting constructs and come to things [new individual difference conceptions] that would make more sense from a neurobiological standpoint," he said.

There are several reasons for incorporating physiology into individual differences assessments, Patrick said. First, many of the major contemporary trait-dispositional models refer to neurobiology, but the neurobiological referents tend to be added after the fact. That is, the traits used in these models were initially developed on the basis of self-report data, and it was only afterward that researchers sought to identify their neurobiological counterparts. By contrast, the psychoneurometric approach seeks to incorporate neurobiological indicators from the beginning so that the trait conceptions themselves are shaped by neurobiological data.

Patrick gave two other reasons for incorporating physiology into the assessment of individual differences: (1) to help address the issue of response bias (which refers to the tendency of people answering questions to be influenced by what they believe the questioner expects), and (2) to gain insight into the processes involved in how people confront and cope with a given situation. The old model of understanding behavior in a situation, the stimulus–response model, was superseded by the stimulus–organism–response model, in which processes occurring within the organism are considered crucial for understanding the connection between the stimulus and the response. Biology is an important part of understanding such relationships. Finally, Patrick noted that understanding the physiological basis of capabilities is important to the design of optimal training performance methods.

Before introducing the two main constructs that he studies, Patrick offered two key points in thinking about the psychoneurometric approach. First, neurobiological indicators of any type are complex and multidetermined. In particular, the reliable person-variance in any physiological indicator will reflect sources other than just the performance capability of interest. And second, linking the domains of physiology and adaptive performance requires a bridge of some sort. The bridging approach he employs is the use of *neurobehavioral constructs*, by which he means "constructs that have clear referents in both neurobiology and behavior." Constructs of this type can serve as referents for combining physiological indicators with indicators from other domains (e.g., self-report or overt behavioral responses) to form composite measures that have meaning both psychologically and physiologically.

Defensive Reactivity

Patrick's work in psychoneurometrics to date has focused on two neurobehavioral constructs. The first is *defensive reactivity*, which he defined as "proneness to negative emotional reactivity in the face of threat." It is a cue-specific negative response, he emphasized, in contrast to, for instance, a free-floating anxiety or neuroticism—that is, the sort of worry or negative emotion that has no obvious immediate cause or trigger.

The presumed neural basis of defensive reactivity is "individual differences in the sensitivity or responsiveness of the brain's defensive system, including the amygdala and affiliated structures." The amygdala is a part of the brain that plays a key role in the processing of cues signaling uncertainty or danger and in the formation of memories of events that have emotional content, such as the memory of a frightening event. Defensive reactivity may also involve interactions with frontal cortical systems of the brain, he said, in terms of what we think of as emotion regulation or inhibition. Frontal cortical brain regions are involved with, among other things, the representation of complex emotional cues or contexts, the formation of long-term memories associated with emotions, and control (regulation) of affective responses.

Patrick's operational model of defensive reactivity—that is, the specific way in which he measures it in human subjects—is based on measures that have been developed to index variations in fear versus fearlessness (or boldness). The model was based on an analysis of data from 2,500 twin participants who completed self-report questionnaires whose scores have been shown in experimental studies to be related to fear-potentiated startle. This fear-potentiated startle is a standard physiological indicator of fear that is often, in practice, the observation of an eye blink in response to some unexpected stimulus, such as a loud noise (Kramer et al., 2012). Figure 3-1 shows how the model represents dispositional fear versus boldness as the common individual difference dimension indexed by differing scale measures of fear/fearlessness.

"We found evidence for a general factor [or dimension] on which all of these measures either loaded positively or negatively," Patrick said. (Two measures are positively correlated when increases in one are associated with increases in the other; they are negatively correlated when an increase in one is associated with a decrease in the other.) Some of the measures Patrick discussed reflect the expression of fear versus boldness in the social domain; others reflect such expression in the activity preference or the sensation-seeking domain, and still others reflect expression in the perceived experience (feeling) domain. "From the standpoint of this model," he said, "we think of neurobiological fear as the core of expres-

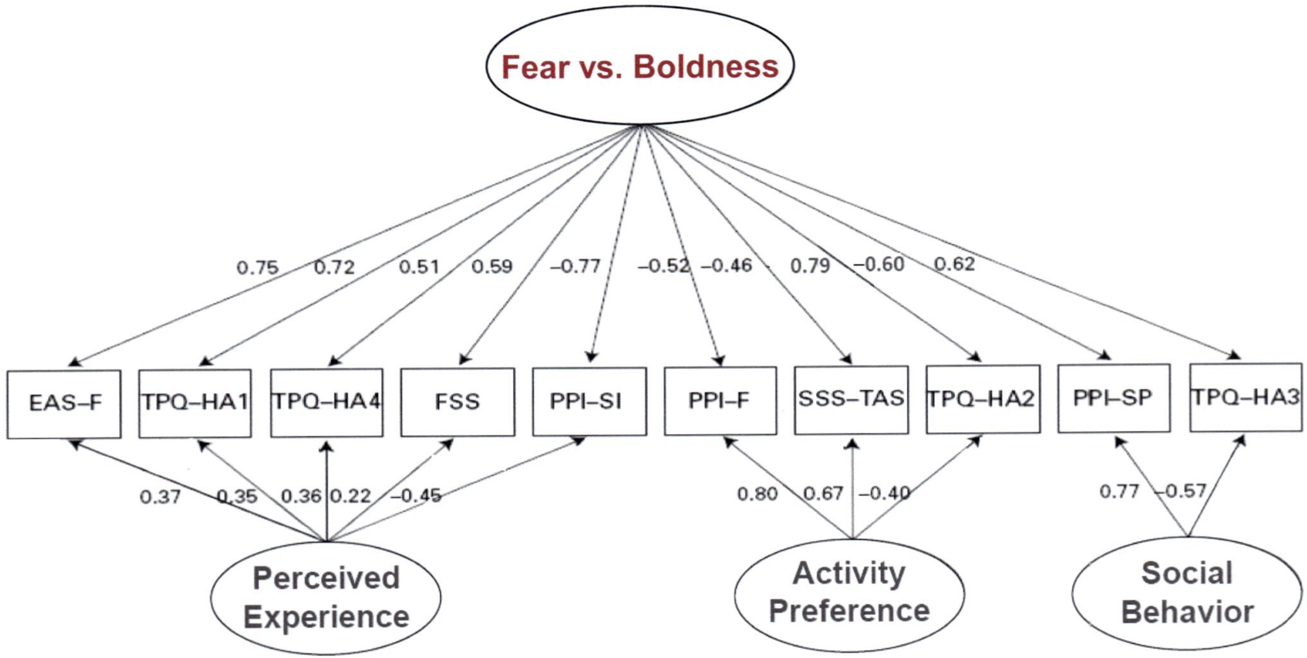

FIGURE 3-1 Operational model: trait fear versus boldness.
NOTE: EAS-F = emotionality–activity–sociability fearfulness scale; FSS = fear survey schedule-III; PPI = psychopathic personality inventory (F = fearlessness subscale, SI = stress immunity subscale, SP = social potency subscale); SSS-TAS = sensation seeking scale, thrill and adventure seeking subscale; TPQ-HA = tridimensional personality questionnaire, harm avoidance scale (HA1 = anticipatory worry and pessimism subscale, HA2 = fear of uncertainty subscale, HA3 = shyness with strangers subscale, HA4 = fatigability and asthenia subscale).
SOURCE: Adapted from Kramer et al. (2012).

sion of fear in different domains, as manifested in self-report, that might hang together separately for other reasons than the physiology of those characteristics." That is, this "dispositional fear" can be thought of as the degree of defensive reactivity exhibited in different psychological contexts; these contexts may seem separate in personality models based on self-report, but from a neurobiological standpoint, the behavior in each context is influenced by variations in dispositional fear. Patrick added that he and his colleagues have followed up on this quantitative modeling work to develop fine-grained scales for measuring the general fear versus boldness dimension of the model using self-reports. They are also interested in measuring the construct behaviorally with various tasks as well as with physiological measures. "Again," he reiterated, "we are choosing these indicators because of their relationship to a neurophysiological indicator," that is, to the fear-potentiated startle response. Thus assessment techniques framed around this model are grounded in neurophysiology.

Applying his ideas to real-world scenarios, Patrick said the trait characteristic of low dispositional fear or "boldness" was well illustrated by the recent article, "Fearless Dominance and the U.S. Presidency: Implications of Psychopathic Personality Traits for Successful and Unsuccessful Leadership" (Lilienfeld et al., 2012). The authors had expert presidential biographers rate the presidents on facet-level traits of the Big Five personality traits model. Based on prior work linking Big Five personality traits to measures of psychopathy, the authors then used these facet ratings to estimate scores for the presidents on factors of psychopathy, one of which, "fearless dominance," is very similar to his own concept of boldness, Patrick said. Among the U.S. presidents considered in the article, Theodore Roosevelt was rated highest in boldness.

In his book *The Antisocial Personalities*, David Lykken writes, "The hero and the psychopath are twigs on the same genetic branch" (Lykken, 1995). The idea, Patrick explained, is that some people may possess the temperament of a psychopath, but because of other factors they do great things. "Lykken talked about the bold tendencies of Winston Churchill as an example of someone who had what he saw as the temperament of a psychopathic individual, but expressed in a more benign sort of adaptive way." What is the difference between someone who expresses this characteristic of boldness adaptively versus maladaptively? Part of the answer, Patrick said, may be found in the second trait he has been studying—inhibitory control.

Inhibitory Control

The second construct on which Patrick's research focuses is *inhibitory control,* which is defined as "the ability to restrain or modulate impulses." This trait relates to the degree to which people can modulate their tendencies and their behavior under conditions that require a certain amount of flexibility and foresight. The presumed neural basis for inhibitory control lies in individual differences in the functioning of anterior brain circuitry, including the prefrontal cortex subdivisions and the anterior cingulate cortex. The operational model for inhibitory control is what he refers to as the "externalizing spectrum," or "trait inhibition–disinhibition" model (Krueger et al., 2007). The sample that Patrick and his colleagues used to develop the model consisted of students as well as prisoners "because we wanted to make sure that we mapped the full range of the continuum by including representations of individuals with very extreme externalizing tendencies."

Again, as with defensive reactivity, the goals of this work were to develop an individual difference measure that had physiological correlates and to develop effective and efficient scales for measuring this construct through self-reports. The model they developed contains 23 facet scales that represent proclivities toward impulsiveness, aggression, rebelliousness, risk taking, and use and abuse of substances, all of which correlate with a broad inhibition–disinhibition factor (Krueger et al., 2007). In this case, the physiological correlates of the inhibition–disinhibition factor include the P300 response and the error-related negativity response, which are two types of brain reactions that can be detected and recorded using the technique of electroencephalography that records brain electrical activity from the scalp surface.

The Value of the Constructs

Patrick gave three reasons why the constructs of defensive reactivity and inhibitory control may be of interest to those developing assessments for military personnel: (1) adaptive performance, (2) direct brain referents, and (3) insights from psychoneurometrics.

Importance to Adaptive Performance

The first reason why these constructs may be of interest for military assessments is that they are important to adaptive performance. For example, a 2009 study found that individuals who were high in boldness were better able to maintain their focus on a task under threat of a shock (Dvorak-Bertscha et al., 2009). Thus it is reasonable to predict that high boldness would predict enhanced adaptive flexibility in a threatening situation.

Responding to a question regarding the distribution of boldness across the population, Patrick indicated that it shows a normal distribution very similar to the levels of intelligence within the population. He also noted that lack of inhibitory control has been shown to correlate with a propensity to develop post-traumatic stress disorder (PTSD) (Miller et al., 2006). He also speculated that, while individuals with high inhibitory control may still develop PTSD, the presence of inhibitory control is likely to produce a more focused and contained reaction to the specific event, rather than manifesting as generalized fear.

Similar to boldness, inhibitory control—which can be assessed via self-report—also correlates with performance in a variety of contexts. Miyake and Friedman (2012) showed, for example, that variations in general executive function contribute to success on a range of different cognitive performance tasks. A 2009 study of twins by Young and colleagues showed performance on tasks indicative of general executive function correlated with scores on the aforementioned inhibition-disinhibition factor (c.f., Krueger et al., 2007), and operationalized by the presence or absence of tendencies toward antisocial behavior and substance abuse. That is, the less inhibited participants were (as evidenced by clinical problems), the poorer they performed on the cognitive tasks related to executive function.

The Constructs Have Direct Brain Referents

The second point Patrick made about the constructs of defensive reactivity and inhibitory control is that they have direct brain referents. A major physiological indicator of boldness, for example, is fear-potentiated startle, which is defined as the increase in the magnitude of the natural defensive startle reflex (generally to a loud noise) that occurs when a person is doing something or viewing something that is scary. People who score high on boldness measures exhibit a reduced fear-potentiated startle, which indicates that they are not so likely to automatically mobilize their defenses in the face of a threat—a characteristic that may be valuable in contexts involving stress or uncertainty.

Similarly, there are various established neurophysiological indicators of disinhibition. One of these is the P300 response, which occurs in response to certain types of stimuli during tasks when a subject is asked to respond selectively to certain stimuli within a series—that is, to respond to some and not to others. The P300 has been studied since the 1980s as an indicator of alcohol problems, Patrick said, and more recently it has been shown to be an indicator of the inhibition–disinhibition dimension that undergirds impulse problems more broadly. Another brain activity–based indicator of inhibition–disinhibition is error-related negativity, a negative deflection in brain activity that occurs when the subject realizes a performance error has been made. Highly disinhibited individuals have smaller responses of this sort, which suggests that they may not be as aware of errors as they occur—a factor that likely contributes to repetition of mistakes.

Patrick's main message in describing this research is that it is possible to investigate—and in the process, clarify—the nature of these individual difference constructs through use of indicators that are purely neurophysiological or by using physiological indicators together with indicators from other domains, such as self-reports or behavioral responses.

The Constructs Can Be Sharpened with Psychoneurometrics

The third reason that constructs of these types are interesting and valuable, Patrick said, is because they have one foot in the domain of psychometrics, the field of psychological measurements, and the other in the domain of neurobiology. This makes it possible to work back and forth between the two domains to sharpen the operationalizations of the constructs and to gain greater insight into their structures and relationships.

In closing, Patrick described a general research strategy that could be useful to achieve this sharpening of individual difference constructs, consisting of the following steps: (1) identify replicable neurophysiological indicators of psychometric measures of target constructs (e.g., disinhibition and trait fear measures); (2) evaluate the covariation among the neurophysiological indicators, that is, identify coherent neurophysiological factors; and (3) revise the psychometric measures and trait conceptions to cohere better with the neurophysiological factors. "The construct and the way we think about it are movable, as a function of what we learn about the convergence of the physiological indicators," he explained. "This allows for psychological trait conceptions to be reshaped by physiological data. Then the revisions to the psychological trait conceptions in turn can help to reshape [one's] conceptions of performance capacities to better accommodate physiological data." The process can be carried out iteratively, sharpening both the psychometric measures and the corresponding physiological indicators.

WORKING MEMORY CAPACITY AND EXECUTIVE ATTENTION

While Christopher Patrick, the first speaker of the Emerging Constructs and Theory panel, focused on the use of neurobiology in measuring and refining constructs, Michael Kane focused on constructs derived from psychological theory. Kane, a professor of psychology at the University of North Carolina at Greensboro, described two such constructs—

working memory capacity and executive attention—that are measurable and predictive of a number of outcomes relevant to the military.

Working Memory Capacity

The construct of working memory capacity, Kane said, is derived from basic cognitive theory and, in particular, from Baddeley's theory of working memory as a complex system that has several storage structures that hold specific types of short-term memories (the phonological loop for the sounds of language, the visuospatial sketchpad for visual and spatial information, and the episodic buffer for various other short-term memories) combined with a "central executive" that controls where attention is focused and coordinates different cognitive processes. The short-term memory structures are closely associated with the corresponding structures for long-term or secondary memory, which consequently have implications for performance. Figure 3-2 illustrates Baddeley's model of working memory.

"The theory is very functionally based," Kane said. "The idea is that working memory evolved for a purpose, which is to help us maintain access to memory representations in the service of ongoing cognitive activities, like comprehending language or solving multistep problems."

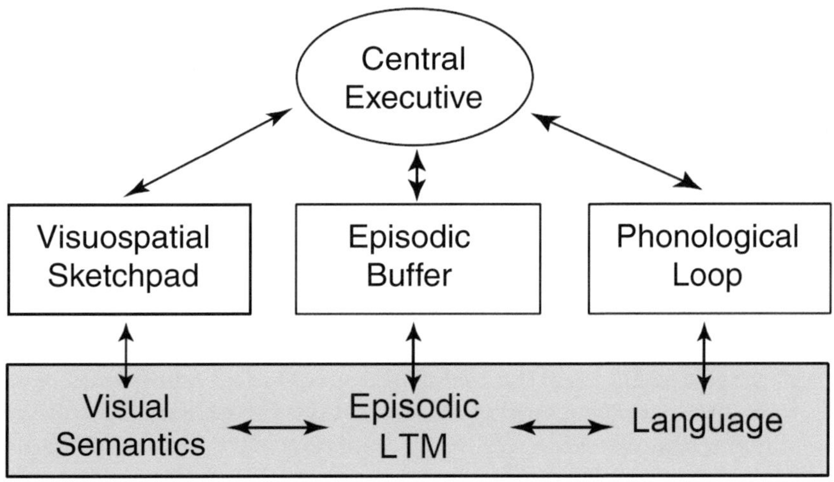

FIGURE 3-2 Baddeley model of working memory.
NOTE: LTM = long-term memory.
SOURCE: Reprinted from Baddeley, A.D. (2000). The episodic buffer: A new component of working memory? *Trends of Cognitive Science,* 4(11):417-423. With permission from Elsevier.

According to Kane, the most compelling evidence for the functional importance of working memory capacity has come from research into individual differences.

For example, research by Daneman and Carpenter (1980) demonstrated that language comprehension capabilities were strongly predicted by students' working memory span scores. A decade later, broad working memory capacity was shown to be an almost perfect predictor of Air Force recruits' general reasoning capabilities (Kyllonen and Christal, 1990).

"Most of the modern research on working memory capacity uses some version of a working memory span task," Kane continued. These are variations on the traditional short-term memory span tasks, which ask subjects to recall item lists in serial order, with the added feature that the items to be remembered are presented alternatively with a secondary processing task, such as judging sentences or verifying equations. The distinguishing feature of the working memory capacity test is that the subjects must "maintain ready access to the goal-relevant information—the memory items—in the face of massive proactive interference from prior trials and attention shifts away from those memoranda as they shift to the processing tasks."

Executive Attention

Not surprisingly, there is a great deal of overlap between measures of working memory capacity and measures of short-term memory and various cognitive abilities. For example, a span task that involves equations will leverage mathematical ability in addition to working memory capacity, and a test that involves mental rotations will reflect spatial ability as well as working memory. By using a series of different types of tests, along with latent-variable analyses, it is possible to tease out working memory capacity from other factors, Kane explained.

In one key example of this type of study, Engle and colleagues (1999) looked at the relationships between memory and reasoning by having their subjects complete three verbal measures of working memory capacity, three span measures of short-term memory capacity, and two nonverbal measures of general fluid intelligence. In this way they could assess commonalities between working memory and short-term memory as well as distinctions between the two. They discovered that memory storage in itself was not correlated with general intelligence. "Rather, it was what working memory did independently, over and above the memory storage demands, that was the strongest predictor of general fluid intelligence." From the point of view of Baddeley's model, it was not the storage system that was key to general intelligence but rather the "attentional executive capability"—the attention-directing part of the system that came to the fore in the memory tests involving multiple tasks—that was most closely associated with fluid intelligence. Kane referred to this capacity as *executive attention*.

Kane went on to describe several studies that demonstrate the roles that executive attention plays, including its relationship to working memory. In one study, he asked subjects to learn and then recall three lists of words, all from the same category, such as "animals" (see Figure 3-3). In some cases they were required to divide their attention by tapping a novel finger sequence on a keyboard over and over again, either while they studied each list (encoding load) or while they tried to recall each list (retrieval load) (Kane and Engle, 2000). Part a of Figure 3-3 shows the results for subjects whose attention was not divided. Subjects with high-working memory capacity (high span) and subjects with low-working memory capacity (low span) recalled approximately the same number of words on the first list, but a clear difference emerged on recall of words on the second and third lists. Both the high span and low span subjects recalled fewer words from the second list and even fewer from the third, but the drop-off was much more dramatic among the low span subjects. The explanation, Kane said, is that those with higher working memory capacity were better able to deal with the "interference" of having to memorize and retain the earlier groups of words.

Interestingly, when the high span subjects were asked to memorize or recall the lists of words while having to divide their attention, their performance (shown in part b of Figure 3-3) dropped to the level of the low span subjects, when not required to divide their attention (shown in part a of Figure 3-3). "Essentially," Kane said, "dividing attention turns high-working memory subjects into functional low-working memory subjects." Thus the test is not just assessing memory. "It is attention that really seems to matter," Kane observed.

This difference in ability to focus attention between subjects with high or low working memory was reinforced in a second study performed by Kane and colleagues (2001) that examined something quite different from memory. In this case high- and low-working memory subjects were tested on how quickly they could move their eyes in the proper direction after a stimulus. It is a standard assessment of executive control referred to as the antisaccade/prosaccade task. (A saccade is a quick movement of the eye.)

"In the prosaccade task," Kane explained, "you stare at a computer screen, wait for a flash on one side of the screen, and look at it. Right there, there is going to be a letter that you have to identify. This is easy. The flash pulls attention toward the cue." The antisaccade version is more difficult: When the light flashes, the subject is instructed to direct his or her vision to the opposite side of the screen to see the target letter. Because this antisaccade movement goes against natural tendencies, everyone is

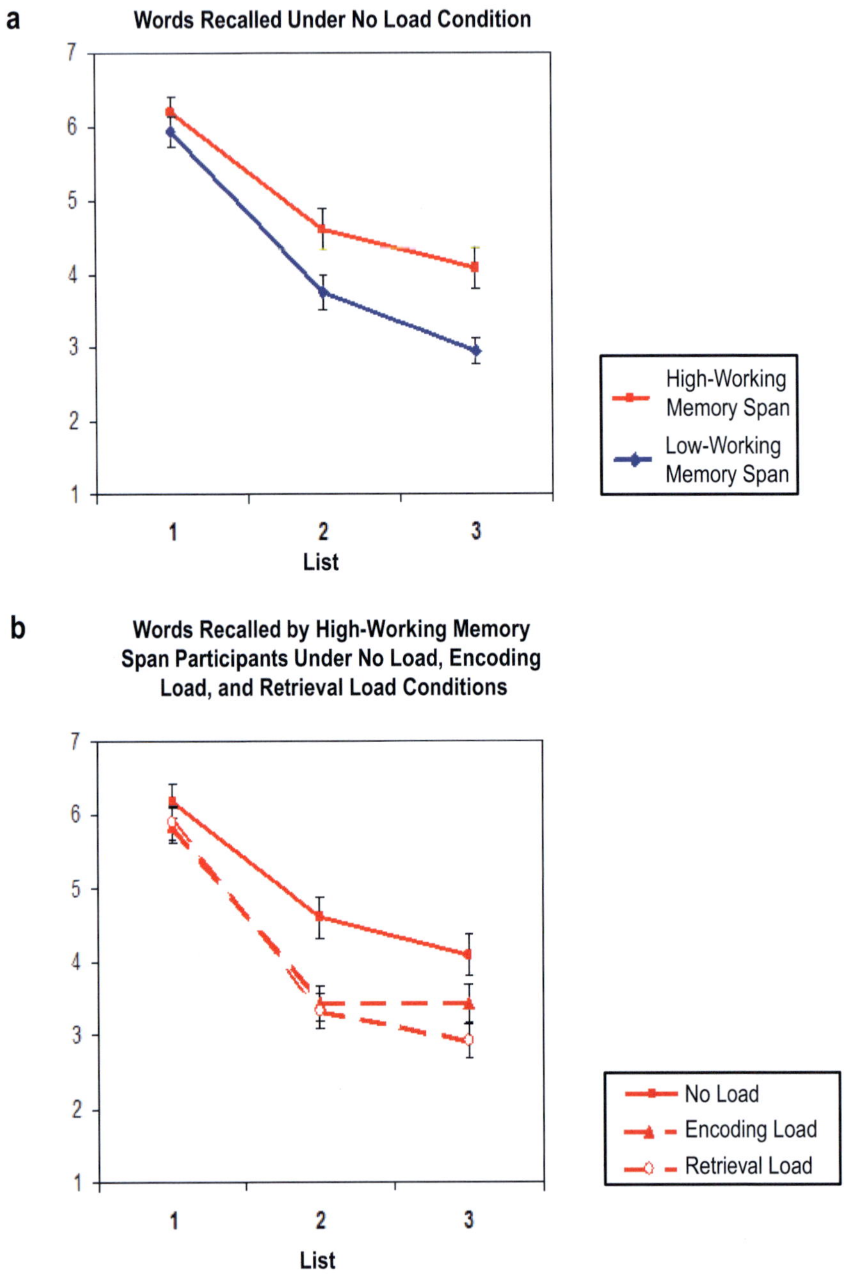

FIGURE 3-3 Working memory capacity and executive attention in a word recall task.
SOURCE: Adapted from Kane and Engle (2000).

slower at this task than at the prosaccade task. The difference in response times between the prosaccade and antisaccade tasks gives a measure of executive control—in particular, how well a subject can control his or her attention.

In their study, Kane and his colleagues found that there was no difference in how quickly the low-working memory capacity (low span) subjects and the high-working memory capacity (high span) subjects responded in the prosaccade task. However, there was a sharp difference between the two on the antisaccade task. Both groups were significantly slower than on the prosaccade task, but the response time was much slower for the low-working memory (low span) subjects (see Figure 3-4).

To explore the phenomenon in greater detail, Kane's group gave the subjects hundreds of trials on the antisaccade task and tracked their eye movements to see where they were looking—and, in particular, to see how often they first looked in the wrong direction, reflexively looking at the flash instead of in the opposite direction. The low-working memory subjects consistently looked in the wrong direction more often than the high-working memory subjects, even after many, many chances to practice and improve (Kane et al., 2001).

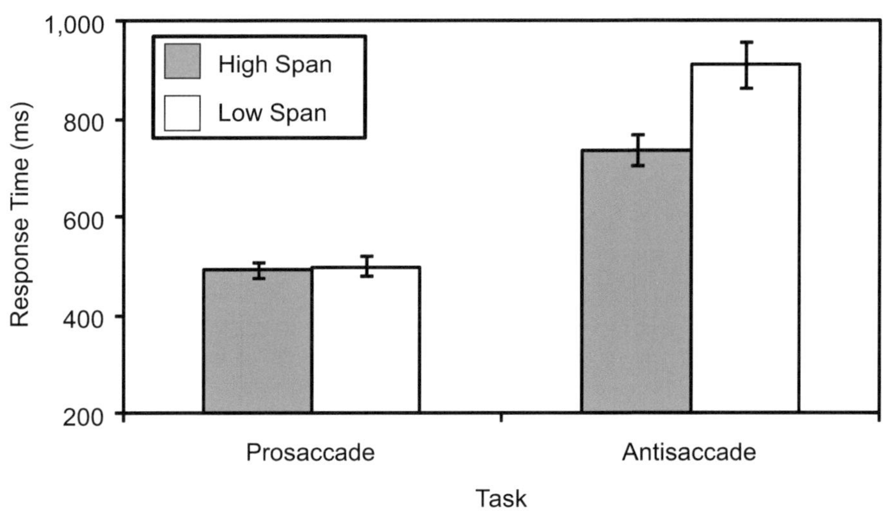

FIGURE 3-4 Working memory capacity and executive attention in prosaccade and antisaccade tasks.
NOTE: ms = milliseconds.
SOURCE: Reprinted with permission from Kane, M.J., M.K. Bleckley, A.R.A. Conway, and R.W. Engel. (2001). A controlled-attention view of working memory capacity. *Journal of Experimental Psychology: General,* 130(2):169-183.

"Remember, there is nothing to memorize in the antisaccade task," Kane said. "There is no word list, it is hardly about memory at all. The only thing to remember is *'look away.'* High-working memory subjects can do that better." Thus the experiment reveals individual differences in the degree of executive control of behavior. High-working memory subjects have greater executive attention and control.

This has some very practical implications, Kane said. For example, the relationship between working memory and restraint over powerful responses has also been seen in both professional police officers (Kleider et al., 2010) and hockey players (Furley and Memmert, 2012). In laboratory-task simulations of real-world scenarios, those members of both groups who had higher working memory capacity made better decisions about whether to shoot or not shoot.

In general, Kane said, research has shown that variation in working memory corresponds to variation in a wide variety of attention-control tasks, including those involving the restraint of some habitual or prepotent response and also those involved in preventing oneself from being distracted by irrelevant stimuli in the environment. One of the more interesting correlations is with multitasking. Kane described a forthcoming study (Redick et al., unpublished) that found multitasking to be a single latent construct; that is, subjects who tested high on one measure of multitasking also tested high on different measures of multitasking, indicating that there is a single underlying ability related to multitasking performance in a variety of areas. Both working memory and attention control were related to multitasking ability, with people who scored better on tests of working memory and attention control also doing better on multitasking tests.

Mind Wandering

In his discussions of attention control, Kane noted that he had focused mainly on subjects who were dealing with external distractors or with controlling overt behavior. But, he said, "the control of attention also works internally, regulating the flow of thought from moment to moment. When that regulation fails, we experience mind wandering, or task-unrelated thinking." So he and his colleagues have been studying mind wandering and how it correlates with working memory capacity and executive attention.

Laboratory studies have shown the tendency for mind wandering to be a stable characteristic (McVay and Kane, 2012; McVay et al., 2009). That is, the subjects who experience more mind wandering while doing one task will also experience more mind wandering while doing another task.

In one study of working memory and mind wandering, Kane and colleagues (2007) first tested a group of students on various working memory tests, then they provided each student with a Palm Pilot personal digital assistant to be kept with the student at all times for one week. The Palm Pilot was programmed to beep eight times a day, at which point the students were asked to report on their conscious experiences and their ongoing activities. In particular, at each beep the students were first asked what they were thinking about at the moment of the beep—were they thinking about what they were doing, or had their minds wandered to something else?

The students were also asked to rate their mood and activities at the time of the beep on a variety of measures. Did they like what they were doing? Was it important? Was it stressful? Each measure was rated on a scale from one to seven. Kane was most interested in three particular ratings that were designed to reflect the cognitive demand of what they were doing: Were they trying to concentrate on what they were doing? Did the activity they were engaged in require a lot of effort? And was the activity challenging? "The idea is that we can get through a lot of life on autopilot," he said. "We don't need to bear down and regulate thought or behavior, except in some circumstances, presumably those characterized by these terms" (i.e., circumstances that are rewarding, important, stressful, or challenging).

When he compared the relationship between mind wandering and how people rated their activities, Kane found a significant negative correlation between working memory capacity and mind wandering—but only on those activities that were rated as challenging or requiring effort or concentration. "As subjects reported trying to concentrate more than usual, being more challenged than usual, or doing tasks that were more effortful than usual, the lower working memory subjects mind-wandered . . . more often than did higher working memory subjects." None of the other contexts—which concerned such things as the subjects' emotions at the time or interest in or importance of the activity—exhibited any interactions with working memory capacity (Kane et al., 2007). It would seem, then, that a higher tendency to mind-wander during challenging tasks indicates lower executive attention. Subjects with high-working memory capacity generally have greater ability to control their attention when they need or choose to. Thus, in situations requiring greater effort or concentration, they were better able to keep their minds from wandering than those subjects with less attention control.

Just as Kane studied how working memory capacity and executive attention interact on a variety of tasks, he also carried out a number of laboratory studies to examine the interplay of working memory and mind wandering to explain various types of performance. In one study, for example, he first tested his subjects on working memory capacity and then had them carry out a 40-minute go/no-go task in which they pressed a button in response to a stimulus over and over again until, occasionally, they were prompted to stop in response to a different stimulus (McVay and Kane, 2009, 2012).

After about 60 percent of the no-go tasks, the subjects were shown a question on a computer screen that asked what they had just been thinking about: the task or a variety of off-task options. The frequency with which one of the options that was not about the task was selected provided a measure of mind wandering.

Also, by measuring the reaction time for each button-push, Kane could observe the consistency of the reaction time over the course of the task. The high-working memory subjects were much more consistent in their reaction times than the low-working memory subjects, who went from "really fast to really slow, all over the map" (see Figure 3-5 for an example of reaction time patterns of two randomly selected high-working memory subjects and two randomly selected low-working memory subjects).

The question then became whether the greater variation in response times among the low-working memory subjects was due to their greater propensity to mind-wander. Kane found that, while the tendency to mind-wander did explain a significant amount of the greater variation in response times, and much of this variation was shared with working memory capacity, working memory capacity also had an effect that was independent of the tendency to mind-wander (McVay and Kane, 2009, 2012). The lesson, he said, is that it is possible to learn more about what subjects are doing and why they are performing well versus poorly by looking at both measures—working memory capacity and tendency to mind-wander—rather than just one.

Similarly, Kane has studied the effects of working memory and mind wandering on reading comprehension. Previous studies had shown that people with greater working memory capacity tend to have better reading comprehension, but the natural question was: How much of that difference is due to differences in the tendency to mind-wander? Kane's studies found that mind-wandering tendencies actually explain somewhat more about reading comprehension than working memory does, but, again, both play a role (McVay and Kane, 2012).

In a more recent, not yet published study, Kane and colleagues have done a similar analysis of working memory capacity, mind-wandering tendencies, and schizotypy, which is a "complex personality structure that confers risk for developing schizophrenia and related psychotic disorders in adulthood" (Kane et al., unpublished). Schizotypy is characterized, Kane explained, by such things as "magical ideation, weird perceptual experiences, difficulty understanding things and being understood by others, and feelings of paranoia and suspiciousness." Kane's studies have shown that mind-wandering tendencies have a significant positive cor-

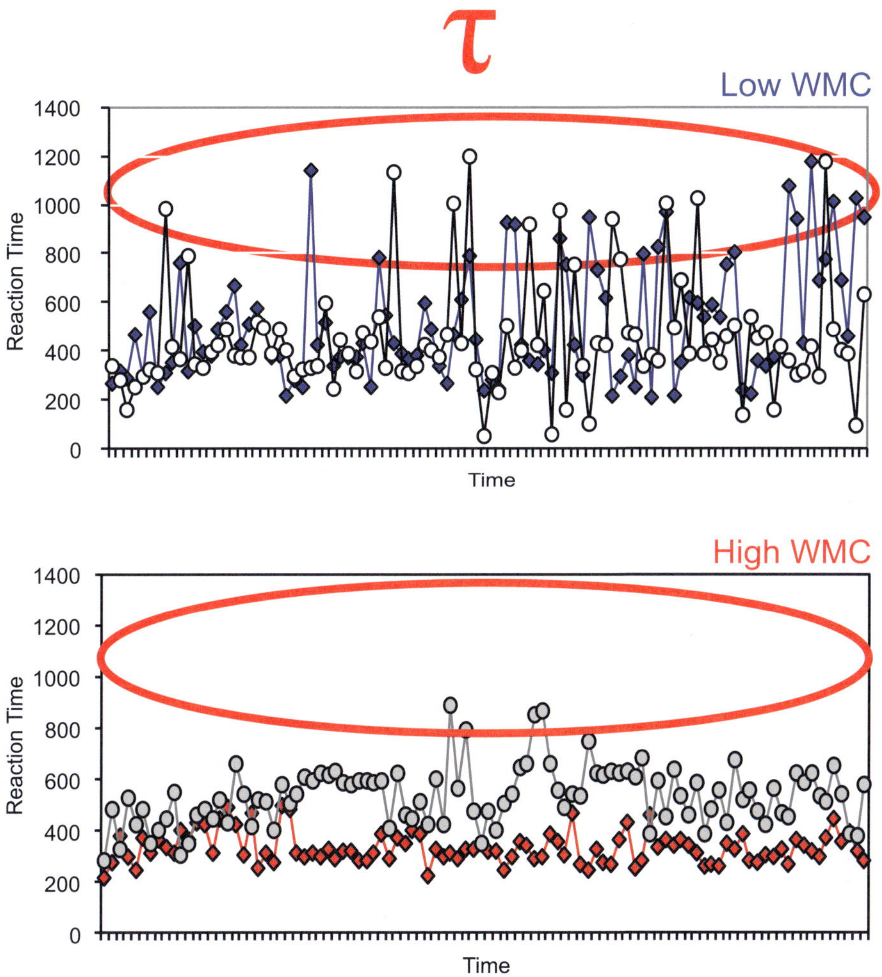

FIGURE 3-5 High- versus low-working memory capacity in go/no-go tasks.
SOURCE: McVay and Kane (2012).

relation with schizotypy. And while working memory capacity also has a significant correlation with schizotypy (negative), it is much weaker. Looking more closely at working memory capacity, Kane found that the pure memory aspect of working memory capacity has no correlation with schizotypy at all; the correlation is completely with the attention-control aspect of working memory (that is, with the variance shared between working memory capacity tasks and lower level attention-control tasks, like the antisaccade task).

To conclude, Kane reiterated the major message of his presentation: "Cognitive psychology can now measure—and is now measuring—theoretically derived, theoretically tractable, and practically important constructs," he said. Working memory capacity and executive attention, which reflect the control of behavior, perception, memory, and thought, are two such constructs, he concluded, and they are predictive of a variety of military-relevant outcomes.

THE AGENTIC SELF: ACTION-CONTROL BELIEFS

In his presentation, Todd Little, professor of psychology and director of the Center for Research Methods and Data Analysis at the University of Kansas in Lawrence, described the action-control model for understanding individuals' beliefs about their own agency, or ability to perform successfully.

Referring to Fred Oswald's presentation, which included a standard theoretical model of core self-evaluation that includes the traits of self-efficacy and locus of control (see Chapter 2), Little explained that his goal was to present an alternative model for thinking about how to measure those kinds of self-related beliefs and expectations about how the world works. From his perspective, he said, both self-efficacy and locus of control are ill-defined concepts, both theoretically and, particularly, operationally. By contrast, action-control theory offers concepts that are easy to operationalize (Little and Wanner, 1997).

To illustrate the difference between the two approaches, Little referred to the "little engine that could" from Watty Piper's classic children's book (1930). The engine's famous line is, "I think I can, I think I can." But, Little said, the line really should have been, "I know *how* one can, I know *what* I can; therefore, I think I can." In other words, the engine's belief is not a simple matter of believing it can do something, but instead it knows how to go about accomplishing the task, and it knows that it has the ability to do that particular thing, so it believes it can accomplish the task. According to Little, that is the action-control model in a nutshell.

Personal Agency

His work is grounded in an organismic perspective, Little said, so he treats most behaviors as volitional and goal-directed. The theory is aimed at understanding actions, and actions are taken as being purposeful, planned, and self-initiated, with a particular goal that the person is trying to achieve (Hawley and Little, 2002; Little, 1998; Little et al., 2006).

In particular, the theory sees individuals as agentic—in conscious control of their behaviors, working toward particular ends. "As agents, we act on our needs and goals," Little said. "We have our intentions, and we interpret and evaluate our actions and their consequences." From watching their own actions, people develop beliefs about their own capabilities. This is the self-regulatory feature of personal agency, he said, "knowing what it takes and whether I've got it."

The Action-Control Model

To illustrate the structure of actions according to his model, Little displayed a figure showing the relationship between the agent, means, and goal (see Figure 3-6). In essence, there is an agent who performs a certain action or means to attain a specific goal, and there are links between each of these constituent parts. The picture is slightly different for an individual thinking about his or her own actions than for an individual thinking about the actions of another.

Agency beliefs are the link between an individual agent and the means that are available to that individual—in the context of the pursued goal. The beliefs are, in essence, an answer to the question "Do I have what it takes?" By contrast, the link between the individual agent and the goal, the *control expectancy*, is the answer to the question "Can I do it?"

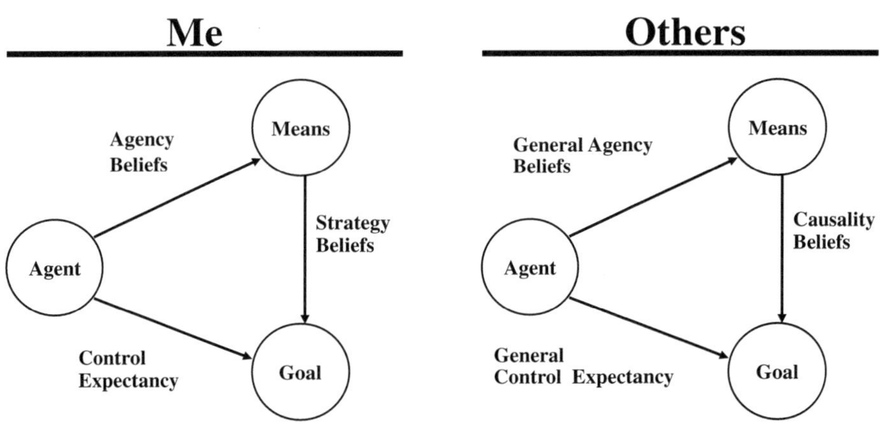

FIGURE 3-6 Action-control beliefs.
NOTE: Means include effort, ability, looks, personality, luck, teachers, parents, peers, etc.
SOURCE: Adapted from Hawley, P.H., and T.D. Little. (2002). Evolutionary and developmental perspectives on the agentic self. In D. Cervone and W. Mischel (Eds.), *Advances in Personality Science*. New York: Guilford Press. Copyright Guilford Press. Reprinted with permission of Guilford Press.

The theoretical definition that Little provided for "agency beliefs" is "Agent (A) has means (M) that is relevant to end (E)." The operational definition is "the person's belief that he or she personally has access to, can use, can implement, or possesses a specific means that is relevant to achieve the outcome." This is where action-control beliefs have an advantage over concepts like efficacy, Little said. "It is a very easy system to operationalize." It is also straightforward to develop specific items to measure agency beliefs, he said. Once the specific context is known, one determines the kinds of means that would be useful in the particular context—being as inclusive as possible—and develops items to assess a person's beliefs about those particular means. Examples of the sorts of items he has used in his own assessments include, "I can try hard," "I am smart enough to do it," "I am unlucky at it," and "I can get others to help me" (see Little and Wanner, 1997).

It is important to note that these are all intrapersonal beliefs—effort, ability, and even luck. "When it comes to the side of agency, luck is an intrapersonal thing," Little said. "It is something that I possess and own, just like my effort and my ability." However, he noted, when an individual evaluates others, luck tends to be interpreted as a factor external to the individual.

Little has studied the relationship between these beliefs and an individual's actual performance in various tasks. He emphasized the striking result that quite often there is no added value to knowing an individual's control expectancy belief—the degree to which an individual believes he or she can achieve the specific goal—versus simply knowing an individual's abilities (Little et al., 1995). "If I know what you possess, in terms of your effort and ability, those will always outperform just whether or not you think you will get it done. The 'I think I can, I think I can, I think I can' doesn't buy us anything in terms of predictive ability."

Similarly, there is generally relatively little correlation between an individual's score on a self-efficacy measure and actual performance (Multon et al., 1991). The correlations between traditional measures of self-efficacy and performance are generally around 0.3, Little said. By contrast, in certain contexts he has seen correlations between action-control beliefs and performance that are greater than 0.7. The key, he said, is refining the measures to be very specific about the goal structure and the specific means that can be used to achieve the goal. The traditional measures of self-efficacy are generally at too high a level of aggregation to be very predictive.

Finally, Little described the *causality beliefs*, or *means–ends beliefs* in his model. "These are really contingent belief operations: my understanding of how the world works; my understanding of, will effort get me to this goal, will ability get me to this goal, will my looks, my personality, teachers, parents, whatever, get me to that goal; and to what degree are they important for achieving that particular goal?" These beliefs develop in a variety of ways, he noted, and they are relatively trainable. "In the school setting, we teach kids what it takes to do well in school. In a military context, we can teach people what it takes to do well in this assignment." Once a person knows what the assignment is, he or she can look for a match between agency beliefs and the causality beliefs.

The important feature here, Little said, is that it is generally possible to provide multiple means to an end, so if a person does not have the tools to do it one way, it can be done another way. For example, a person might think of it this way: "I am not really the sharpest pencil in the box, but I will work . . . and I will just go and go and go and go. I can get to the same goal that you can because you are smart. I can get there by effort."

There are various ways that action-control beliefs are acquired, Little said. Some of them come from direct experiences with success and failure, while others are taught by parents, teachers, peers, and others (Little, 1998). Feedback on one's own performance helps refine the various beliefs, as do vicarious observations: watching and seeing how others do things, in person or virtually.

One important influence on action-control beliefs is social comparisons: a person learning how he or she measures up to others. But the comparisons need to be accurate. In the United States, Little said, "when we ask kids about their agency beliefs for doing well in school, everybody believes they are above average because the teachers keep telling them they are great and wonderful." By contrast, in Germany honest feedback is a "valued cultural aspect," and agency beliefs are much more closely correlated with performance scores (Little et al., 1995; Oettingen et al., 1994).

According to Little, another important influence on action-control beliefs comes from symbolic actions—that is, by thinking through and rehearsing what it would take to carry out a certain task, without actually doing it (Boesch, 1991; Brandstädter, 1998). Using symbolic actions, people can develop action-control beliefs in a completely new context, one with which they have no previous experience.

Little closed by describing some of the differences that have been reported in the literature between agentic and nonagentic people (Hawley and Little, 2002; Little et al., 2006); that is, between those who tend to believe in their ability to control things in their lives and those who do not (see Box 3-1). Nonagentic people have little sense of personal empowerment, feel helpless when they are challenged, and tend to accept failures. They have low aspirations and perform poorly on most tasks. Agentic individuals are just the opposite. They have a greater sense of personal empowerment, they persist in the face of obstacles, and they learn from failures. They have high aspirations and perform well on tasks.

BOX 3-1
Nonagentic Versus Agentic Profiles

Nonagentic Profile	Agentic Profile
• Has low aspirations	• Has high aspirations
• Feels helpless when challenged	• Persists in the face of obstacles
• Is hindered by problem-solving blinders	• Sees more and varied options
• Performs poorly	• Performs well
• Accepts failures	• Learns from failures
• Has greater ill-being	• Has greater well-being
• Has little sense of personal empowerment	• Has a greater sense of personal empowerment

SOURCE: Little presentation.

DISCUSSION

Following the three panel presentations, committee members, the presenters, and other participants engaged in a roundtable discussion that included specific questions for the panelists as well as thought-provoking brainstorming on the future of measurements and assessments. The following section captures some of the more salient ideas expressed during the group discussion.

The first several questions to panelists addressed the distribution of various traits across the population and when certain traits might be more desirable than others. Participants debated in detail the importance of the context of the task in judging desirable traits. For example, when might it be better to be more likely to be distracted from a task (for example, if an emergency happens outside your area of attention) versus being highly focused on the task? In response, Patrick clarified the idea of fear versus boldness as a normal individual difference continuum: "To have a lot of fear is non-normative, but potentially adaptive in certain contexts," he said. Likewise, he continued, to have very limited fear is non-normative but potentially adaptive in other contexts. That is, the existence of individual differences in fearfulness reflects an adaptive trade-off between exploratory types of behaviors and tendencies toward defensive withdrawal. Little agreed with this point, noting that it is not necessarily always the leader who survives; "followers survive, too, when they hook up with the right leaders" (see Hawley 1999; Hawley and Little, 2002; see also Buss and Hawley, 2010, for an edited volume on the evolution of individual differences).

The discussion of the many potential factors contributing to success at a specific task led Little to emphasize that any assessment of potential performance is a "multivariate problem." "Working memory is clearly an important factor," Little said, "but boldness is there, too. How does boldness work with working memory, under which contexts do we see an optimal one? We might find that boldness is selected for in some contexts, whereas memory is in others." Several of the participants suggested that creating performance context, affective context, and other relevant contexts may be an interesting approach to assess the relationships and interactions of many different constructs in different situations. Later, Patrick took the discussion further by suggesting that not only should some things be assessed together but other things may need to be dissociated. Assessments may thus need to strategically separate constructs, to determine how they respond as indicators are manipulated. For example, Patrick added, "you are still holding onto something that is, say, callousness, but you are moving it away from disinhibition, so aggression is no longer an indicator." Further proof of the need to both combine and disentangle constructs, according to Patrick, is the existence of suppressor relationships between correlated constructs: predictions improve as clear discriminate relationships emerge.

Stephen Stark, a committee member, asked Little about the context for the beliefs and traits assessed by his model. "There have been studies that suggest that contextualizing personality items seems to increase the predictive validity of the measures," Stark noted, adding that one of the common concerns with generalized contextualization is that contextualizing the items too much may ultimately require different types of items for different situations. From a practical standpoint, this could be a challenge. Stark then asked Little to explain context with regard to his measures and the level of specificity necessary to achieve high validities relative to the broader, higher-level self-efficacy constructs and locus of control. In particular, Stark said that there are different occupational specialties in the military and that recent work suggests that different personality profiles are more or less predictive of performance across different jobs. He asked how specific the items would have to be in Little's tool to be useful for at least families of jobs that are fairly similar in terms of their goals, characteristics, and environments.

Little responded that he believed his tool could be effective at the level of job families such as military occupation specialties. "I could see a level of aggregation for these beliefs, that you would still have predictive capability, but wouldn't necessarily have to get down to specific job title." He also thought it may be possible to have more refined tools that could determine which of two jobs in a particular job family a candidate might be best suited for. "You do the big sweep, you get your low-hanging fruit first," he said. "Then, you start doing follow-up assessments, after you can start moving people in the right direction, and then you can get to specific components."

INTERESTS

In his presentation during the workshop's second-day panel of individual differences and performance, James Rounds, a professor of psychology and educational psychology at the University of Illinois at Urbana-Champaign, further contributed to the workshop's theme of emerging constructs and theory. Rounds began by suggesting that the future of individual performance prediction should revisit its history. In the 1920s and 1930s, psychologists paid a great deal of attention to personal interests in the belief that they would be predictive of many things, including how successful people would be in their careers. However, over time that attention faded as evidence seemed to indicate that interests had relatively little predictive power. However, Rounds argued that it is time to give interests a second look. Not only are interests surprisingly stable over the course of a person's life, he said, but, when analyzed properly, they can also be used to predict performance and achievement.

Rounds then offered some background on how interests are generally approached by psychologists, describing two approaches to studying interests. One approach considers interests in terms of situations, that is, as context-specific "emotional states, curiosity, and momentary motivation" (Schraw and Lehman, 2001). This approach is associated more with educational psychology and with an experimental approach to interests. It is generally referred to as "situational interests" or sometimes "individual interests."

The other approach, generally referred to as "dispositional interests," considers interests more in terms of personal traits that reflect a person's "preferences for behaviors, situations, contexts in which activities occur, and/or the outcomes associated with the preferred activities" (Rounds, 1995). In other words, interests are seen as expressions of underlying personality traits.

Generally speaking, Rounds said, researchers who study situational interests do not collaborate with those who study dispositional interests, to the extent that they might even be considered two separate scientific disciplines. They do not share data or ideas, and each group is generally unaware of the other group's work. Thus, according to Rounds, some things have fallen between the cracks.

Some of the earliest work in the field was done by people in the dispositional interest camp. In the 1920s, Walter Bingham set in motion a program that eventually led to the development of nine different interest inventories—sets of questions designed to identify interests in various areas. One of these inventories, developed by Edward K. Strong, Jr. (1943) is still used today. The underlying assumption in much of this work, according to Rounds, is that understanding interests would lead to a better understanding of performance.

However, in recent years the more predominant assumption has been that interests actually have relatively little to do with performance. Much of the change, Rounds said, can be traced to a paper published in 1984 by Hunter and Hunter, who reported that there was very little correlation between interests and performance—generally no more than about a 0.1 correlation. Other studies used the evidence from that paper to suggest that interests are not effective predictors of performance (for example, Barrick and Mount, 2005). The result, Rounds said, is that "you will not find anyone talking about performance and interests, period." Furthermore, "you hardly find interests in textbooks anymore." But Rounds believes that there is a great deal to learn from studying interests, and he offered three lines of evidence, summarized below, to support his contention.

Interests and Performance

Much of what has been written about interests, Rounds said, discusses interests as a motivational type of variable. It provides some sort of direction, it energizes a person, and it increases persistence (Nye et al., 2012).

There is also a parallel literature on person–environment fit (see, for example, Kristof-Brown et al., 2005, and Verquer et al., 2003). That literature suggests that the extent of compatibility between an individual and his or her environment can influence performance outcomes. Unfortunately, Rounds said, much of that literature ignores interests. Yet he believes that the literature on person–environment fit has the potential to show interests in a different, more compelling light.

To show why, Rounds described a meta-analysis that he and colleagues conducted on 60 studies published since 1934 (Nye et al., 2012). Of those 60 studies, 45 percent were published after the Hunter and Hunter paper appeared in 1984. The analysis included both studies that used interest scale scores and studies that used congruence indices reflecting the fit between a person's interest profile and either the person's job or the person's occupational profile. The authors tested for correlations between the interest scores or congruence and several measures of performance, including task performance, organizational citizenship behavior, persistence in the workplace, and persistence and grades in an academic setting.

The analysis found a clear correlation between interests and performance, no matter how performance was measured. The overall correlation was 0.20—about double what Hunter and Hunter had reported nearly three decades earlier. What was most striking, however, was the overall correlation between performance and the congruence indices—about 0.36, which was very significant (Nye et al., 2012). Thus, while interests are moderate predictors of performance criteria, the correlations increase substantially when the congruence between the individual's interests and the environment is considered.

The takeaway message, Rounds said, is that fit, particularly with regard to interests, really matters.

Interests and Career Success

A second study from Rounds' laboratory looked at the incremental validity of vocational interests beyond personality and cognitive abilities in predicting academic achievement and career success (Su, 2012). It involved the analysis of data from a large-scale longitudinal study, Project Talent, which began in 1960. Five percent of American high school students in grades 9 through 12 participated in a full 2 days of testing, which included a comprehensive set of cognitive ability measures, 10 personality scales, and a large collection of interest items. After the original testing, the participants were surveyed 3 additional times—at 1, 5, and 11 years after their high school graduation—about their educational, occupational, and personal development.

Rounds' graduate student performing the study, Rong Su, used regression analysis to determine the relative importance of interests, personality, and ability for various types of achievements, such as college degrees attained and income. Su found that ability was clearly important and that, indeed, it was the most important predictor of every achievement except income. Personality also played a role, but interests played a larger role than personality in every area, and interests were by far the biggest predictor of income (Su, 2012). The results are shown in Figure 3-7.

It is natural to assume, Rounds noted, that the correlation between interests and income can be explained by people selecting jobs in better-paying fields, such as science or business, but the data indicate it is not that simple. "The predictive power of interests for income does not just come from its influence on career choices," he said, "but also comes from its influence on advancement in a career."

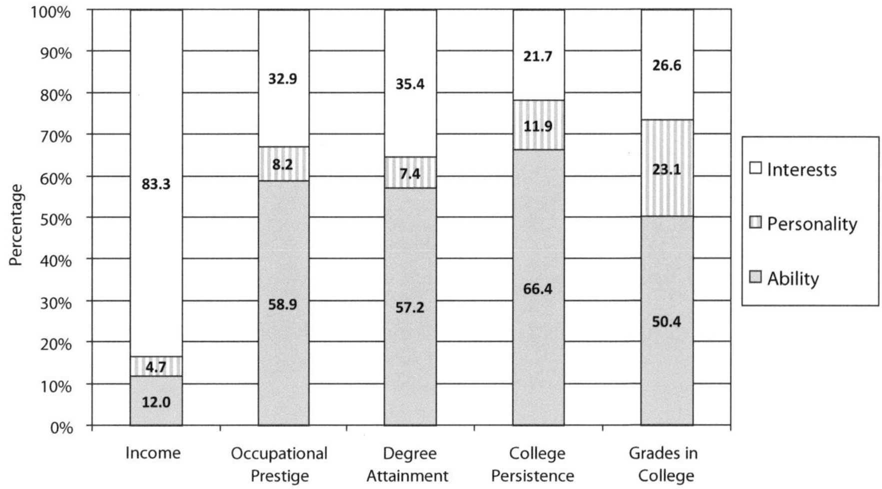

FIGURE 3-7 Relative importance of interests, personality, and ability for educational and career success.
SOURCE: Adapted from Su (2012, p. 126).

The Stability of Interests

Interests have always been considered fairly stable, Rounds said, but no one had looked carefully at exactly when they become stable and how they might change, for example, from adolescence to young adulthood. To investigate the stability of interests, Rounds and his colleagues carried out a meta-analysis of 66 studies (Low et al., 2005). They found there were few studies that examined the stability of interests beyond age 40. However, they were able to access a significant amount of data concerning the stability of vocational interests from ages 12 to 40.

The analysis found that there was a big jump in stability of interests at about age 18, at which point they stabilize and stay about the same through age 40 (Low et al., 2005). This finding is important, Rounds said, because it indicates interests stabilize much earlier in life than had previously been thought. It is also useful information for predictive purposes, since one can reasonably assume that whatever measures of interest are obtained for subjects after age 18 are likely to remain fairly stable.

One surprising result of the study, Rounds said, concerned the stability of interests versus the stability of personality. Most researchers tend to think of things like interests and values as deriving from basic personality traits, and so it would seem that interests should be less stable than personality traits. However, the data indicated that interests are substantially more stable than personality traits (Low et al., 2005).

REFERENCES

Baddeley, A.D. (2000). The episodic buffer: A new component of working memory? *Trends of Cognitive Science*, 4(11):417-423.

Barrick, M.B., and M.K. Mount. (2005). Yes, personality matters: Moving on to more important matters. *Human Performance*, 18(4):359-372.

Boesch, E.E. (1991). *Symbolic Action Theory and Cultural Psychology.* Berlin, Germany: Springer-Verlag.

Brandstädter, J. (1998). Action perspectives on human development. In W. Damon (Series Ed.) and R. Lerner (Vol. Ed.), *Handbook of Child Psychology: Vol. 1. Theoretical Models of Human Development* (pp. 1029-1144). New York: Wiley.

Buss, D.M., and P.H. Hawley (Eds.). (2010). *The Evolution of Personality and Individual Differences.* New York: Oxford University Press.

Daneman, M., and P.A. Carpenter. (1980). Individual differences in working memory and reading. *Journal of Verbal Learning and Verbal Behavior,* 19(4):450-466.

Dvorak-Bertscha, J.D., J.J. Curtin, T.J. Rubinstein, and J.P. Newman. (2009). Psychopathic traits moderate the interaction between cognitive and affective processing. *Psychophysiology*, 46(5):913-921.

Engle, R.W., S.W. Tuholski, J.E. Laughlin, and A.R.A. Conway. (1999). Working memory, short-term memory, and general fluid intelligence: A latent variable model approach. *Journal of Experimental Psychology: General*, 128(3):309-331.

Furley, P.A., and D. Memmert. (2012). Working memory capacity as controlled attention in tactical decision making. *Journal of Sport and Exercise Psychology,* 34(3):322-344.

Hawley, P.H. (1999). The ontogenesis of social dominance: A strategy-based evolutionary perspective. *Developmental Review*, 19(1):97-132.

Hawley, P.H., and T.D. Little. (2002). Evolutionary and developmental perspectives on the agentic self. In D. Cervone and W. Mischel (Eds.), *Advances in Personality Science* (vol. 1, pp. 177-195). New York: Guilford Press.

Hunter, J., and R.F. Hunter. (1984). Validity and utility of alternative predictors of job performance. *Psychological Bulletin*, 96(1):72-98.

Kane, M.J., and R.W. Engle. (2000). Working memory capacity, proactive interference, and divided attention: Limits on long-term memory retrieval. *Journal of Experimental Psychology: Learning, Memory, and Cognition*, 26(2):336-358.

Kane, M.J., M.K. Bleckley, A.R.A. Conway, and R.W. Engle. (2001). A controlled-attention view of working-memory capacity. *Journal of Experimental Psychology: General,* 130(2):169-183.

Kane, M.J., L.H. Brown, J.C. McVay, I. Myin-Germeys, P.J. Silvia, and T.R. Kwapil. (2007). For whom the mind wanders, and when: An experience-sampling study of working memory and executive control in daily life. *Psychological Science*, 18(7):614-621.

Kane, M.J., T.K. Kwapil, and P.J. Silvia. (unpublished). Executive Control and Schizotypy in the Laboratory and Daily Life. National Institute of Mental Health-funded R15 project (MH 093771-01).

Kleider, H.M., D.J. Parrott, and T.Z. King. (2010). Shooting behaviour: How working memory and negative emotionality influence police officer shoot decisions. *Applied Cognitive Psychology*, 24(5):707-717.

Kramer, M.D., C.J. Patrick, R.F. Krueger, and M. Gasperi. (2012). Delineating physiologic defensive reactivity in the domain of self-report: Phenotypic and etiologic structure of dispositional fear. *Psychological Medicine*, 42(6):1305-1320.

Kristof-Brown, A.L., R.D. Zimmerman, and E.C. Johnson. (2005). Consequences of individuals' fit at work: A meta-analysis of person-job, person-organization, person-group, and person-supervisor fit. *Personnel Psychology,* 58(2):281-342.

Krueger, R.F., K.E. Markon, C.J. Patrick, S.D. Benning, and M. Kramer. (2007). Linking antisocial behavior, substance use, and personality: An integrative quantitative model of the adult externalizing spectrum. *Journal of Abnormal Psychology,* 116(4):645-666.

Kyllonen, P.C., and R.E. Christal. (1990). Reasoning ability is (little more than) working-memory capacity?! *Intelligence,* 14(4):389-433.

Lilienfeld, S.O., I.D. Waldman, K. Landfield, A.L. Watts, S. Rubenzer, and T.R. Faschingbauer. (2012). Fearless dominance and the U.S. presidency: Implications of psychopathic personality traits for successful and unsuccessful political leadership. *Journal of Personality and Social Psychology,* 103(3):489-505.

Little, T.D. (1998). Sociocultural influences on the development of children's action-control beliefs. In J. Heckhausen and C.S. Dweck (Eds.), *Motivation and Self-Regulation Across the Life Span* (pp. 281-315). New York: Cambridge University Press.

Little, T.D., and B. Wanner. (1997). *The Multi-CAM: A Multidimensional Instrument to Assess Children's Action-Control Motives, Beliefs, and Behaviors* (Materialen aus der Bildungsforschung, Nr. 59, ISBN #3-87985-064-x). Berlin, Germany: Max Planck Institute for Human Development.

Little, T.D., G. Oettingen, A. Stetsenko, and P.B. Baltes. (1995). Children's action-control beliefs about school performance: How do American children compare with German and Russian children? *Journal of Personality and Social Psychology*, 69(4):686-700.

Little, T.D., C.R. Snyder, and M. Wehmeyer. (2006). The agentic self: On the nature and origins of personal agency across the lifespan. In D.K. Mroczek and T.D. Little (Eds.), *Handbook of Personality Development* (pp. 61-79). Mahwah, NJ: Lawrence Erlbaum Associates.

Low, K.S.D., M. Yoon, B.W. Roberts, and J. Rounds. (2005). The stability of vocational interests from early adolescence to middle adulthood: A quantitative review of longitudinal studies. *Psychological Bulletin,* 131(5):713-737.

Lykken, D.T. (1995). *The Antisocial Personalities*. Hillsdale, NJ: Lawrence Erlbaum Associates.

McVay, J.C., and M.J. Kane. (2009). Conducting the train of thought: Working memory capacity, goal neglect, and mind wandering in an executive-control task. *Journal of Experimental Psychology: Learning, Memory, and Cognition,* 35(1):196-204.

McVay, J.C., and M.J. Kane. (2012). Drifting from slow to "d'oh!": Working memory capacity and mind wandering predict extreme reaction times and executive control errors. *Journal of Experimental Psychology: Learning, Memory, and Cognition,* 38(3):525-549.

McVay, J.C., M.J. Kane, and T.R. Kwapil. (2009). Tracking the train of thought from the laboratory into everyday life: An experience-sampling study of mind wandering across controlled and ecological contexts. *Psychonomic Bulletin and Review,* 16(5): 857-863.

Miller, M.W., D.S. Vogt, S.L. Mozley, D.G. Kaloupek, and T.M. Keane. (2006). PTSD and substance-related problems: The mediating roles of disconstraint and negative emotionality. *Journal of Abnormal Psychology*, 115(2):369-379.

Miyake, A., and N.P. Friedman. (2012). The nature and organization of individual differences in executive functions: Four general conclusions. *Current Directions in Psychological Science,* 21(1):8-14.

Multon, K.D., S.D. Brown, and R.W. Lent. (1991). Relation of self-efficacy beliefs to academic outcomes: A meta-analytic investigation. *Journal of Counseling Psychology,* 38(1):30-38.

Nye, C.D., R. Su, J. Rounds, and F. Drasgow. (2012). Vocational interests and performance: A quantitative summary of over 60 years of research. *Perspectives on Psychological Science,* 7(4):384-403.

Oettingen, G., T.D. Little, U. Lindenberger, and P.B. Baltes. (1994). Causality, agency, and control beliefs in East versus West Berlin children: A natural experiment on the role of context. *Journal of Personality and Social Psychology,* 66(3):579-595.

Piper, W. (1930). *The Little Engine That Could.* New York: Platt and Munk.

Redick, T., Z. Shipstead, M. Meier, J. Evans, K. Hicks, N. Unsworth, M. Kane, Z. Hambrick, and R. Engle. (unpublished). Understanding the Role of Working Memory Capacity in Complex Task Performance to Improve Sailor and Marine Selection, Classification, and Training. Office of Naval Research project.

Rounds, J.B. (1995). Vocational interests: Evaluation of structural hypotheses. In D. Lubinski and R.V. Dawis (Eds.), *Assessing Individual Differences in Human Behavior: New Concepts, Methods, and Findings* (pp. 177-232). Palo Alto, CA: Consulting Psychologists Press.

Schraw, G., and S. Lehman. (2001). Situational interest: A review of the literature and directions for future research. *Educational Psychology Review,* 13(1):23-52.

Strong, E.K., Jr. (1943). *Vocational Interests of Men and Women.* Palo Alto, CA: Stanford University Press.

Su, R. (2012). The Power of Vocational Interests and Interest Congruence in Predicting Career Success. Dissertation, University of Illinois at Urbana-Champaign. Available: https://www.ideals.illinois.edu/bitstream/handle/2142/34329/Su_Rong.pdf?sequence=1 [June 2013].

Verquer, M.L., T.A. Beehr, and S.H. Wagner. (2003). A meta-analysis of relations between person-organization fit and work attitudes. *Journal of Vocational Behavior,* 63(3):473-489.

Young, S.E., N.P. Friedman, A. Miyake, E.G. Willcutt, R.P. Corley, B.C. Haberstick, and J.K. Hewitt. (2009). Behavioral disinhibition: Liability for externalizing spectrum disorders and its genetic and environmental relation to response inhibition across adolescence. *Journal of Abnormal Psychology,* 118(1):117-130.

4

Emerging Understandings of Group-Related Characteristics

In the military, as in most other modern organizations, little work is done by individuals working alone. Thus it is important to be able to assess individuals not only on the basis of their individual performance potential but also on the basis of how their characteristics might operate in a group setting. During the second day of the workshop, the third panel, Group Composition Processes and Performance, was devoted specifically to issues related to assessments that can provide insights into group performance and the effective assembly of groups. Invited presentations from Anita Williams Woolley, Scott Tannenbaum, and Leslie DeChurch included discussion of the "collective intelligence" of a team, how to assess and predict team performance, and how best to assemble teams.

COLLECTIVE INTELLIGENCE

To begin her presentation, Anita Williams Woolley, an assistant professor of organizational behavior and theory from Carnegie Mellon University, described various types of animals that exhibit "collective intelligence"—memory or problem-solving behaviors that are the product of an interaction among members of the group rather than simply a reflection of the capabilities of the individual members. Ant colonies, Woolley said, provide one of the best examples in that individual ants are simple creatures with little memory or problem-solving ability, but collectively they exhibit impressive behavior. They create complex structures, for example, and they locate sources of food and assign collection priority according to distance from the nest.

After these introductory observations, Woolley described her research on collective intelligence in groups of people. She began her research program with two specific questions: (1) Is there evidence that groups of people have some form of collective intelligence—a product of collaboration within the group that goes beyond what the group's members can accomplish individually? (2) If collective intelligence exists, is it something that transcends domains—that is, if a group excels in one area or on one type of task, is it likely to excel in other areas or on other tasks? Her research shows that the answer to both questions is a clear "Yes" (Woolley et al., 2010).

Collective intelligence, Woolley explained, can be thought of as a group version of the general intelligence factor, *g*, for individuals. The existence of *g*, which was originally hypothesized by Charles Spearman (1904) in the early part of the 20th century, can be inferred from the fact that people who do well on one type of task also tend to do well on other types of tasks (Deary, 2000). The idea behind *g*, Woolley said, is that it is a capability that is not specific to a particular domain but rather one that transcends domains. Similarly, if it could be shown that groups that do well on one type of task also tend to do well on other types of tasks, then one could infer the existence of a collective intelligence, *c*, associated with groups. Woolley and her colleagues initiated a research program to investigate this hypothesis.

In particular, Woolley said, there were several specific questions that she sought to answer with her research:

- Is there evidence of a general collective intelligence (*c*) in groups?
- Can we isolate a small set of tasks that is predictive of group performance on a broader range of more complex tasks?
- Does *c* have predictive validity beyond the individual intelligence of group members?
- How can we use this information to build a better science of groups?

Woolley hoped it might be possible to develop tests for collective intelligence in groups that played a role similar to intelligence quotient (IQ) tests for individuals—that is, tests that sample from a relatively small number of domains but that generalize to a broader set of domains and thus could provide a relatively convenient way of predicting the likely performance of groups on a large variety of tasks.

Woolley's first study to investigate the possible existence of a collective intelligence involved 40 groups that each spent five or more hours in her lab (Woolley et al., 2010). After a group's members were assessed on individual intelligence and a number of other characteristics, the group worked together on a range of tasks and also, after the tasks, on a video game simulation to provide a collective measurement of performance.

The tasks were divided into four types: (1) *generating* tasks, which consisted of such things as brainstorming sessions and which benefited from a variety of inputs so as to devise more creative solutions; (2) *choosing* tasks, typical decision-making tasks in which the group needed to identify the individual who had the right answer to a question; (3) *negotiating* tasks, which involved trading off against competing interests to come up with a solution that best suited the group as a whole; and (4) *executing* tasks, which required careful coordination of inputs to accomplish goals quickly and accurately. Each type of task required a fundamentally different approach for the group to perform at a high level, Woolley explained, so there was no obvious reason to assume that a group that was good at one task, such as brainstorming, would also be good at another task, such as figuring out which group member knew the right answer for a decision-making task.

Nonetheless, analysis of the data from the 40 groups found a clear correlation between performances on different tasks, Woolley reported, such that a group that did well on one task type was more likely to do well on another. "We also had a first-principle component that accounted for 43 percent of the variance," Woolley said, "which compares favorably to IQ tests, where the first component generally accounts for between 30 and 50 percent of the variance." When they carried out a confirmatory factor analysis on the data, they found clear evidence that a single factor explained the relationships among the tasks better than a multifactor solution, and, furthermore, that a single general factor of collective intelligence was also a strong predictor of how the groups performed later on the criterion task (Woolley et al., 2010). Most importantly, Woolley emphasized, the collective intelligence factor did a far better job of predicting performance on the video game simulation than did the IQ of the individual group members. "We modeled this in terms of the maximum IQ score, the average IQ score, et cetera," Woolley said, "and it didn't really add any explanatory value to our model." Later she repeated the study with a larger sample, a broader range of group sizes, and a different criterion task, and she found very similar results: The collective group intelligence, as determined from the range of tasks, was much more predictive of performance on the criterion task than the IQ scores of the individual group members (Woolley et al., 2010).

In later studies she investigated how well collective intelligence predicted group learning (Aggarwal et al., unpublished). It is well known that individual intelligence predicts learning, she noted. "So we were interested to see whether this would be true at the group level as well."

To test this idea, Woolley assembled about 100 teams to study. After administering the collective intelligence tests to each of the teams, the teams played a number of rounds of a behavioral economics game in which the goal is to earn as much money as possible. After each round, the team received feedback about how much money it had earned. As shown in Figure 4-1, on average, the groups with low collective intelligence improved very little through 10 rounds of the game, while the groups with high collective intelligence improved greatly in terms of the amount of money they earned.

Additionally, Woolley and her colleagues looked at teams of students in a Master's program in business administration, who work together on projects over the course of a term (Aggarwal et al., unpublished). The students took four different exams as a team, with the individual members first taking each exam individually and then repeating the same exam with their group, without first receiving feedback on their individual performances (the dashed lines in Figure 4-2 illustrate the highest individual score obtained in each team). The teams with low collective intelligence and those with high collective intelligence scored almost equivalently on the first group exam. However, as the solid lines in Figure 4-2 illustrate, while teams with either high or low collective intelligence improved,

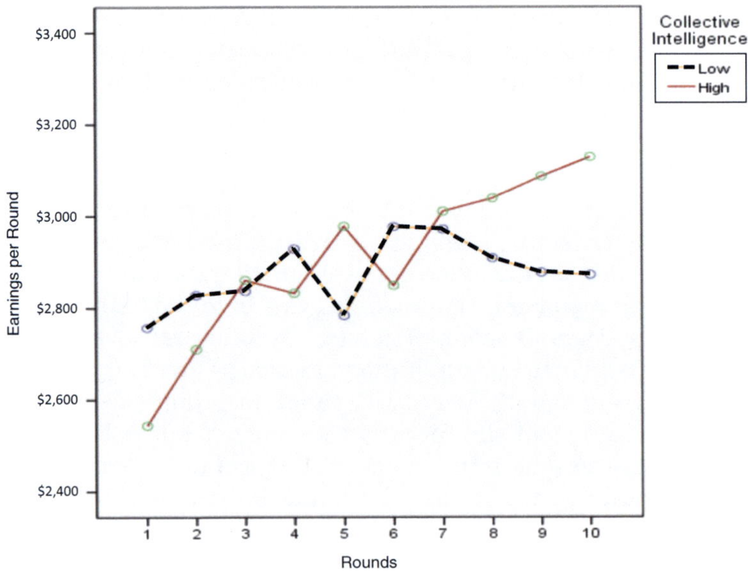

FIGURE 4-1 Collective intelligence and learning as measured in a behavioral economics game.
SOURCE: Adapted from Aggarwal et al. (unpublished).

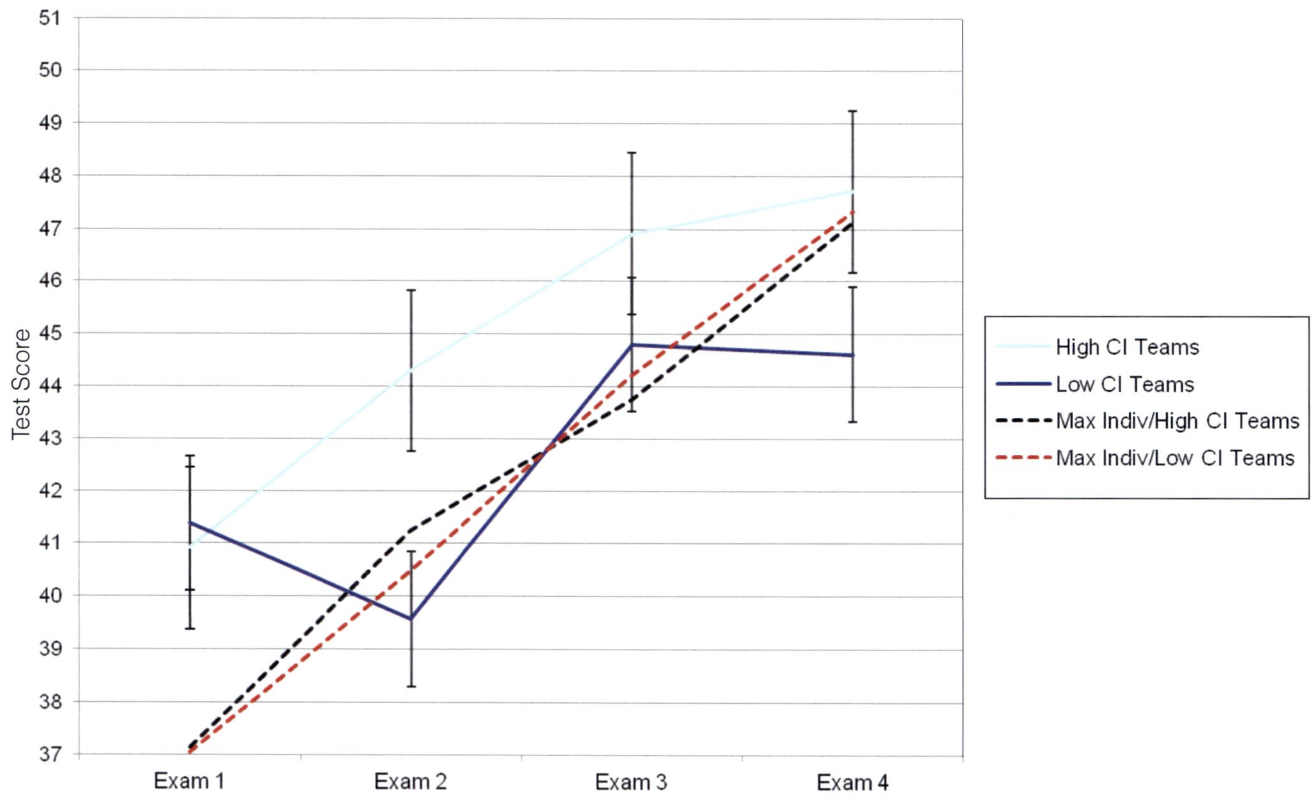

FIGURE 4-2 Collective intelligence (CI) in classroom teams.
SOURCE: Adapted from Aggarwal et al. (unpublished).

by the fourth group exam, the teams with high collective intelligence improved significantly more and outscored the teams with low collective intelligence. Woolley noted that, when the group scores (solid lines in Figure 4-2) were compared with the highest individual score on each team (dashed lines in Figure 4-2), the teams with low collective intelligence scored no better than their best team member 50 percent of the time, while the teams with high collective intelligence consistently scored significantly better than their best team member.

Since the collective intelligence of these teams depends on more than the intelligence of their individual members, Woolley said, the question is what factors influence collective intelligence. Or, in other words, what are the best predictors of collective intelligence?

"We've administered a variety of measures of group climate, things like group satisfaction, cohesion, or motivation, and have not found any significant relationships [with collective intelligence]," Woolley said. "We've administered a variety of personality measures, largely based on the Big Five [personality traits], . . . and we haven't found consistent relationships with personality." However, she said, one predictor of collective intelligence that has emerged repeatedly in her studies is the proportion of females in the group. Judging from data collected from other studies, the relationship is a curvilinear one (see Figure 4-3). Groups with a low percentage of women tend to show lower collective intelligence than groups consisting solely of men. Whereas groups with more than about 20 percent females in the group up to about 75 to 80 percent female display increasing collective intelligence. The trend reverses above 80 percent females and collective intelligence drops slightly as the percentage approaches 100.

This trend is consistent with research done by Myaskovsky and colleagues (2005), Woolley said. What they found, Woolley explained, is that in groups with just one female, you often don't hear much from them. Whereas in groups with only one male, you actually hear a lot from the women, so the amount of communication overall in the groups that are predominately female is much greater than in groups that are predominantly male (Myaskovsky et al., 2005).

A second factor that is predictive of collective intelligence, Woolley noted, is the social perceptiveness of the group's members. This can be measured with a simple test that asks the test taker to select one of four options that best describes the mental state of a person shown in a photograph, but limited to only showing the person's eyes. People who are more socially perceptive are more accurate in inferring mental states from these narrow-view photographs (Baren-Cohen et al., 2001). Woolley found that groups whose members have a higher average score on social perceptiveness also tend to have higher collective intelligence. Because women

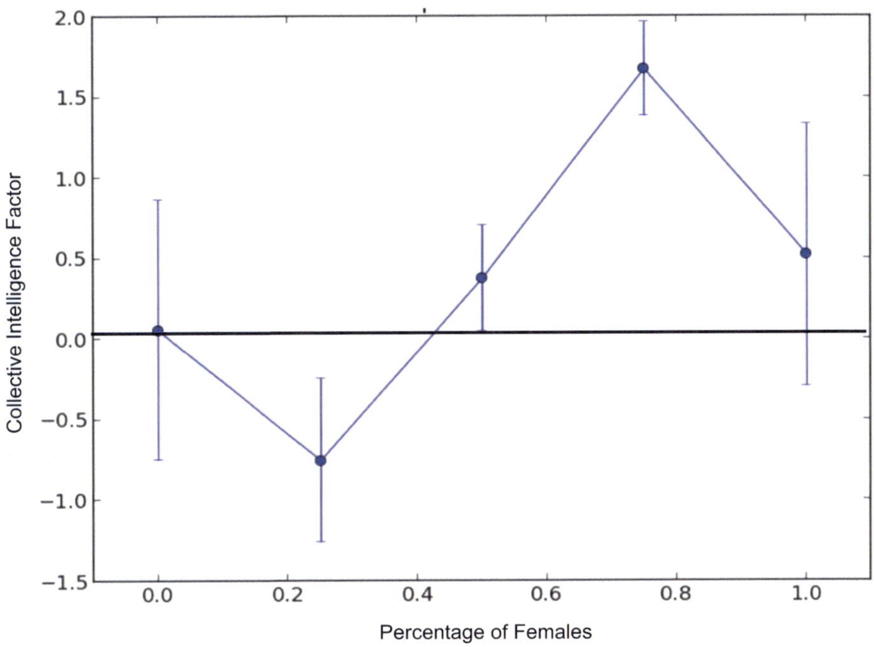

FIGURE 4-3 Relationship between collective intelligence and the percentage of females in the group.
SOURCE: Adapted from Engel et al. (unpublished).

tend to score higher on social perceptiveness, having more women in a group will generally raise its average social perceptiveness score, Woolley said, which explains most, but not all of the effects associated with the proportion of women in the group.

By studying communication in these groups, Woolley has also found that uneven distribution in speaking turns is negatively correlated with collective intelligence, so groups in which one person dominates the conversation tend to have lower collective intelligence (Woolley et al., 2010). "We found it was true even for online groups that were communicating by chat only," she said (Engel et al., unpublished).

She has also examined the effects of cognitive diversity on collective intelligence. There are various cognitive styles, she noted. Some people are verbalizers, while others are visualizers. Among visualizers, some are better with objects, while others are better with spatial patterns. When she examined the relationship between diversity of cognitive styles and collective intelligence, Woolley found a curvilinear pattern: Collective intelligence tends to increase as the cognitive diversity of a group increases, but only up to a point; once a group gets too cognitively diverse, its collective intelligence tends to drop. Groups that are highly diverse in cognitive styles tend to experience difficulty communicating and arriving at agreement on strategies to deal with different problems because they are fundamentally different in the way they think and approach a task (Aggarwal and Woolley, 2013).

Looking ahead, Woolley said, she is interested in discovering what else predicts collective intelligence. She has also been working to refine her battery of tests so that it can be used in other environments to predict team performance and also so that it can be used to experiment with tools that enhance various processes that improve collective intelligence.

Discussion: Collective Intelligence in Online Groups

In the discussion period following her presentation, Woolley noted that she had recently finished a study comparing face-to-face teams with online teams and found that the pattern of relationships still held. "Surprisingly," she said, "the proportion of women is even more influential in the online teams than in the face-to-face teams, even when they are anonymous and they don't necessarily know that the other people are male or female."

Gender information is not provided explicitly to online team members, but, Woolley noted, the team members assign themselves chat names, which may or may not indicate their sex. If a team member assigned herself a name that is clearly feminine, she said, then other team members could guess that she was a woman.

Committee member Randall Engle commented that Woolley's results indicate that the collective intelligence of the group is dependent on the number of females in the group, even when the group members themselves do not know how many females are in the group. This raises the possibility, he observed, of doing some interesting experiments in which the team members' perceptions of their teammates could be manipulated to study, for instance, whether the belief that the team was mostly male or mostly female might make a difference to performance.

Woolley responded that she has some collaborators who have been manipulating perceptions of cultural background rather than of gender, so that while everyone in the group is American, the group members are led to believe that some of their teammates are Arabs. They have found that such perceptions do indeed affect the group's collective intelligence.

Furthermore, Woolley said, social perceptiveness is even more influential in the online teams than in the face-to-face teams. Rodney Lowman, who led the discussion on ethical implications at the end of the workshop's first day, pointed out that while Woolley described measuring social perceptiveness in the lab with visual tests that ask a subject to determine a person's emotional state from looking at a picture of the person's eyes, people have no such visual data to work with online. "That's correct," Woolley responded, adding that conceptually this measure of social perceptiveness is tapping into "theory of mind": the ability to represent to oneself another person's mental states based on subtle cues. "What it suggests," Woolley noted, "is that the measure generalizes to other modes than simply the visual identification of emotional expression."

PREDICTING TEAM PERFORMANCE

To a certain degree, well-qualified individuals are more likely to perform well as a team on various tasks, relative to a team of less-qualified individuals. However, as Woolley's work on collective intelligence found, individual characteristics tell only part of the story (Woolley et al., 2010). Other factors also play a role in team effectiveness. The question, then, is what those factors are and how to predict the effectiveness of a team from the characteristics of its individual members. Scott Tannenbaum, president and cofounder of The Group for Organizational Effectiveness, Inc., discussed this issue in his presentation on team composition.

Modeling Team Composition

Tannenbaum began with a discussion of theoretical considerations. Noting that there are many different approaches to putting together an effective team, he described a simple classification system as a way of imposing some order on the variety of approaches. In his system, there are four types of team composition models (see Table 4-1).

The first and most traditional model, represented by the upper left quadrant in Table 4-1, is the individual selection model, in which individuals are assessed in various ways and then matched to a job. "One way you could think about this," Tannenbaum said, "is that this is about picking individuals who are most qualified to do [a specific] job."

It is also possible to consider individual characteristics that are related to the functioning of a team—that is, characteristics that make a person a good team player. A personnel model with teamwork considerations (upper right quadrant in Table 4-1), Tannenbaum said, seeks to select people based not only on their individual competencies but also on how well they are likely to collaborate and coordinate when working as part of a team. There are many different types of team competencies, Tannenbaum explained, and some of them are generic, meaning that, regardless of what team a person is on and what sorts of tasks the person is asked to do, these competences will help the person be a better team player. For

TABLE 4-1 Four Models of Team Composition Effectiveness

	Individual Focus	Team Focus
Individual Models	**Traditional Personnel—Position Fit Model** *Position-Specific KSAOs* Cognitive Ability Psychomotor Ability Conscientiousness	**Personnel Model with Teamwork Considerations** *Team Generic KSAOs* Organizing Skills Cooperativeness Team Orientation
Team Models	**Relative Contribution Model** *Relative KSAOs* Weakest Member Highest Leader Propensity Cooperativeness of Most Central Person	**Team Profile Model** *KSAOs Distributions* Average Experience Functional Diversity Team Requisite KSAOs

NOTE: KSAOs = knowledge, skills, abilities, and other characteristics.
SOURCE: Reprinted with permission from Mathieu et al. (2013).

example, this might include communications skills, organizational skills, cooperativeness, and team orientation.

These first two types of models are relatively well studied and well accepted, Tannenbaum said; the remaining two types of models are where he expects many future developments. These models approach team composition from the team perspective, rather than from the individual perspective. "This is about thinking about a team member's talent," Tannenbaum said, "but you can't look at it in isolation. It is relative to other people on the team."

For example, consider a team of people working an assembly line. The person with the poorest skills in a particular area will limit the overall team performance. In other cases, the key factor in team performance might be the most positive person or the strongest person, or it might be the level of cooperativeness displayed by the person who is most central to the team's workings. This relative contribution model, represented by the lower left quadrant in Table 4-1, assesses individual characteristics in a team framework.

The most complex model, represented by the lower right quadrant of the table, is the team profile model, which seeks to optimize the blend, synergy, and profiles of the team members. "You take a look at all these pieces simultaneously," Tannenbaum said, and consider the team's collection of skills. So, for example, in some instances it may not matter exactly who performs specific tasks, only that at least one person on the team has the requisite skill and that collectively the team possesses the necessary skills to fulfill the team's mission. It is the overall team profile that matters.

As an aside, Tannenbaum noted that he and his colleagues have been working to create mathematical models that describe the effectiveness of teams under each of these models. The idea, he said, is to show that it is possible to describe these team characteristics with algorithms and not simply in words.

The Team Role Experiences and Orientation Assessment

With this theoretical grounding in place, Tannenbaum described the Team Role Experiences and Orientation (TREO) assessment. "TREO is a measure of team role propensities," he explained. "In other words, in team settings, what is someone likely to do? What do they gravitate toward?" TREO is based on the premise that by understanding people's team-related preferences and interests—what they like to do and what they are interested in when on a team—and by learning about their past behaviors when they were on previous teams, it is possible to predict how they are likely to behave on teams in the future (Mathieu et al., unpublished). With that information in hand, it should be possible to examine the propensities of the different team members to predict the performance of that team more accurately than would be possible simply from knowing about the knowledge, skills, and abilities of the individual team members.

TREO is a 48-item self-assessment that scores people against six roles: organizer, challenger, team builder, doer, innovator, and connector. "These are just what they sound like," Tannenbaum said. "Organizers are people who tend to structure and provide guidance and control over things. Challengers are people who are likely to speak up and question things. Innovators are folks who have new ideas to bring to the table." The doers are "head-down people that will get the work done," while team builders "focus on the morale and engagement of the team," and connectors build bridges with people outside the team.

Using seven different samples, Tannenbaum and his team conducted a confirmatory factor analysis to test the validity and reliability of the TREO constructs, and the results are promising, he reported. They also compared the TREO characteristics with the usual Big Five personality traits and found that, while there are some logical correlations, the TREO characteristics generally do not overlap with the standard personality traits. Tannenbaum said that this makes sense because the Big Five are intended to measure individual personality, while TREO is looking at how people act when they are in team settings. He added, "this is back to some of that contextualization that people were talking about yesterday"—that is, one way to improve assessments is to take context into account instead of simply working with context-free assessments such as the Big Five personality traits.

Tannenbaum and his team have compared the TREO results with measures of teamwork knowledge and with peer assessments, in which they asked team members about the behaviors they had observed in other members. The peer assessments exhibited patterns similar to what TREO indicated, demonstrating a correlation between what people self-reported on the TREO assessment and what others reported about the behaviors they saw exhibited by team members.

At first, Tannenbaum said, it might seem as if the TREO assessment belongs in the upper right quadrant of Table 4-1 because the scores seem to be about individuals and their team-related characteristics. But TREO is better thought of as falling in the bottom half of the figure, he added, where the team composition and profile are emphasized. Imagine, for example, that a TREO assessment of a five-person team indicates that all members score very high on organizing or on challenging; that would be very revealing about the way the team was likely to function—or not function. "Here's where the bang for the buck is, in terms of being able to move things forward," he said.

Although he has done only a few studies testing whether TREO can predict team performance, Tannenbaum views the preliminary data as promising. He briefly described results from three studies, one that looked at 45 Army transition teams and two that used student samples—one with 110 teams doing a simulated aviation task and the other with student teams that worked together over a 10-week period on a variety of tasks (Tannenbaum et al., 2010).

In the student team studies, the students were first tested on individual knowledge, skills, and abilities and then a team profile was created. In one study, the team profile was created using TREO results, and in the other the profile was constructed using personality measures. In both cases, adding the team profile details increased predictive power. In particular, the team profiles were used to predict the effectiveness of various team processes, which the literature shows do a very good job of predicting team performance (Tannenbaum et al., 2010). Adding the team profiles to the information about individual abilities produced better predictions of team processes than information about individual abilities alone, Tannenbaum said. "So the punch line here is that team composite data can account for additional variance above and beyond just looking at individuals."

The results from the study with Army transition teams were somewhat more complex. The teams consisted of soldiers who were together for approximately 16 weeks before they were deployed. "What we found was a compensatory relationship," Tannenbaum said. If a team was low on some individual capabilities but higher on the team profile, the better team profile could make up for some of the lack of individual capabilities. But teams that were low in both areas performed poorly. "So it's not always so straightforward, but yet again there's a relationship showing that we can predict team processes above and beyond that of individual performance" by looking at team composite data in addition to individual data.

TEAM ASSEMBLY

As several participants noted, the ultimate goal of developing an understanding of team performance is to be able to improve team assembly—to put together individuals on teams in a way that maximizes performance. Both Tannenbaum and Leslie DeChurch, an associate professor of organizational psychology at Georgia Institute of Technology, addressed this challenge.

Team Composition System

Tannenbaum described a tool that he and his team developed at The Group for Organizational Effectiveness, Inc., to aid in assembling a team. The tool, called the Team Composition System (TCS), is still in the prototype stage, but Tannenbaum described it to illustrate possible approaches for improving team assembly.

The underlying impetus for developing TCS, he said, was to address the challenge of assembling a team while considering so many different factors that a person could not effectively keep track of them all without help. As examples of the many potentially relevant factors, Tannenbaum cited the knowledge, skills, and abilities of the various candidates; their personality traits and how people will fit together; which abilities are needed on the team; who the weakest link is likely to be for a particular task, and so on. TCS includes the mathematical formulas previously developed to describe the effectiveness of a team in terms of various individual and team characteristics; it also includes input from the TREO assessment. Currently, Tannenbaum said, TCS is designed to build only one team at a time. Optimizing the assembly of multiple teams from a group of candidates requires consideration of so many different possible permutations that it was not practical with the computing power available to him.

Tannenbaum explained that TCS takes a decision maker through a series of six steps:

1. Describe the team.
2. Specify the team requirements.
3. Manage candidate data.
4. Run the analysis.
5. Review the results.
6. Lock in candidates, adjust assumptions, re-run the analysis, decide.

He reiterated that TCS is designed as a decision aid, not a decision maker. It helps guide someone through assembling a team by offering analyses of different potential teams. It shows configurations that are predicted to be most effective based on the assumptions provided, but it does not make the decision for the decision maker. "You can go back, change your assumptions, lock in people, unlock people. This is how decision makers tell us they operate. They don't want a system telling them the answer. They want a system that they can use to have data to help make decisions."

TCS has a number of additional features that increase its flexibility to adjust to the user's needs. For example, it allows users to specify team characteristics in various ways. Depending on the task, some positions on a team may be more important than others; therefore, the system allows positions that are more central to be weighted more in the analysis.

Sometimes there are skill requirements that need to reside in the team but not in an individual position. Tannenbaum offered an example: "I need somebody on the team who speaks Farsi. It doesn't have to be the commander, it doesn't have to be the navigator, but it has to be somebody." Or it might be that a certain number of NATO partners are needed on the team. The system can steadily maintain that requirement while other factors are manipulated. Various other types of constraints can be included as well. Sometimes two people can't work together, for instance. The system can be told to ignore any potential team options with those two individuals as members of the same team.

After all the data are entered, including such things as the TREO assessments of potential team members, the system runs an analysis of all possible team combinations and, based on the various assumptions and constraints that were entered, it identifies the five potential team configurations with the highest predicted team effectiveness scores. It also provides alerts that signal potential problems with each team. It can identify potential weak links, for example, based on individual position readiness scores. Or it might note that more than half the team scores high on the "challenger" scale, which may indicate team members might spend too much time critiquing one another. TCS, as Tannenbaum explained, monitors and manipulates many more factors than any individual could, so it can make the team assembly process more effective and efficient.

Mechanisms and Modalities in Assembling a Team

In her presentation, Leslie DeChurch described a different way of thinking about team assembly. She began by arguing that the current approaches to understanding team effectiveness do not work particularly well. "Over the last 13 years there have been 8 meta-analyses that have desperately looked for significant effect sizes linking team composition, diversity, and capabilities to team performance," she said (see, for example, Stewart, 2006, and Bell et al., 2011). "And basically we don't really know much despite the search for moderator after moderator. The best-case scenario is, we know that if you put smart people on a team [the team tends] to perform better."

There are three important deficiencies in this literature, according to DeChurch. First, the examination of team composition has been too narrow. "We need instead to talk about team assembly," she said. That is, it is not enough to examine the characteristics of the individuals on a team; one must also take into account how the team was put together.

"The second thing," she said, "is that if we want to understand how individual characteristics combine toward collective capability, we have to model the mechanisms. Teams are about relationships." Thus, DeChurch emphasized, it is crucial to examine how people work together—or do not work together—on a team.

Third, DeChurch believes the best effects of individual characteristics on the construction of team capabilities will emerge if one looks at the dyadic or the relational level of analysis. Teams consist of many people, but relationships are generally one on one, and thus, she explained, dyads should be the basic unit of analysis when understanding why some groups work better than others.

Team Assembly Mechanisms

To begin her analysis, DeChurch defined what she meant by "team assembly." "I'm arguing that we need to move outward from thinking about composition as the totality of all the factors that influence the formation of teams," she said. DeChurch explained that currently the literature emphasizes only one level of factors, called team composition, but she believes there are at least four levels that should be considered. She referred to these four levels, or ways of thinking about what is important in determining the functioning of a team, as "team assembly mechanisms," which are illustrated in Figure 4-4.

A Level 1 mechanism considers compositional factors, or what people normally consider when putting together a team: the knowledge, skills, abilities, personality traits, and other individual factors of the team members. Level 2 considers person–task fit, or how the characteristics of the individual team members match up with the tasks the group members will undertake (for example, Keegan et al., 2012). Level 3 examines relational considerations—in particular, the prior relationships that individual team members have had with one another (for example, Guimera et al., 2005). Level 4, the ecosystem level, includes analysis of individuals' previ-

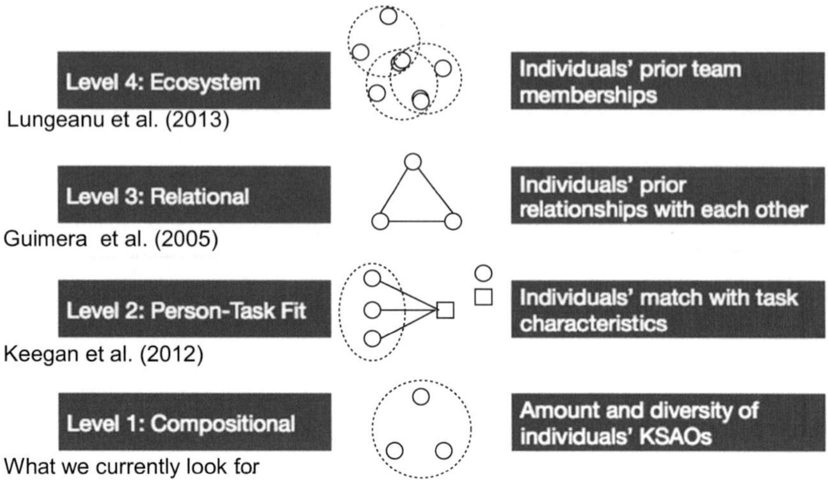

FIGURE 4-4 Team assembly mechanisms.
NOTES: Citations in Figure 4-4 represent examples of studies that consider a factor at each team assembly mechanism level. KSAOs = knowledge, skills, abilities, and other characteristics.
SOURCE: DeChurch presentation.

ous team memberships (for example, Lungeanu et al., 2013). To illustrate Level 4, DeChurch said that two people on a team who were previously members of the same team will take norms and experiences with them into the new team, based on those prior teams. This level goes beyond prior individual relationships, DeChurch continued, "we are only going to see it if we model the ecosystem, which includes current teams in the context of all the teams that have come before them."

Team Assembly Modalities

In addition to examining team assembly mechanisms, DeChurch said that it is also important to understand assembly modalities—that is, the way in which teams are formed. For example, team members can be assigned to various teams, or they can self-organize. "Self-organization can take many subtle forms," she explained. "We can think about the process of an individual applying for a job or a position within a company after having been selected [for the company]. If it is a team-based job, the individual is attempting to self-organize into that team."

A second way to classify assembly modalities is by the amount of information that is available to form the team. She referred to the information as *unstructured* if the team assembly took into account information about the individuals involved but did not consider how the individuals might fit together. On the other hand, if team assembly takes into account information about how potential team members might fit together, it is using *structured information*. Thus, DeChurch said, there are two important factors that arise from the modality of team formation. "One of them is the degree of control and agency that's involved, and the second is the amount of information about the mix of people that's put forth in assembling a team." These two variables define four separate modalities of team assembly, which DeChurch illustrated with Figure 4-5.

Thinking about team assembly in terms of mechanisms and modalities raises a number of research questions, she said. First, how do the modalities affect the mechanisms of assembly? What effect does the amount of available information or the degree of agency have on team assembly mechanisms, team relationships, and, ultimately, team performance? Second, what is the relative impact of the different mechanisms on team processes, states, and performance? Third, what are the intervening variables through which assembly at these four levels comes to impact team performance? And fourth, which individual differences predict preferences for different modalities? In the remainder of her presentation, DeChurch provided preliminary data to answer the first of these suggested research questions.

The Effect of Modality on Team Assembly Mechanisms

To test the effect that modalities have on the fundamentals of how teams form, DeChurch and her colleagues recently carried out an experiment with 95 students who formed into 30 teams, each of which had 3 to 4 members. The experimental teams were composed of psychology students working on a semester-long project that required them to apply

FIGURE 4-5 Team assembly modalities.
SOURCE: DeChurch presentation.

findings on attitude and behavior change to aid in the commercialization of a scientific breakthrough.

The individual students chose how they would assemble into teams, DeChurch explained. "They had three choices. They could allow the instructor to randomly put them on a team, they could self-organize ad hoc, . . . or they could use a tool that we built called the My Dream Team Builder," which was essentially a recommendation system that helped students decide who they might want to be on a team with—that is, data-driven self-organization. Sixty-one of the students chose to use the tool to self-organize, 11 chose ad hoc self-organization (for example, they chose to be on a team with friends), and 23 chose to be randomly assigned. "This resulted in 6 teams in which the dominant modality was assignment, 9 that we'll call blended assembly—they had some level of assignment and some level of self-organization—and 15 that were matched purely using this builder."

Within each team, the investigators measured a variety of Level 1 assembly factors—gender, age, personality, intercultural sensitivity, and so on (for background on factors assessed, see Chen and Starosta, 2000, and Donnellan et al., 2006)—and one Level 3 factor: the individuals' prior social networks. Four weeks after the teams were formed, relationships among teams were measured using sociometric surveys that captured the patterns of communication in a team, the efficacy of communication, people's confidence in their ability to work with each specific member of the team, their trust in the others on the team, and their reliance on one another for leadership of that team.

As a comparison, DeChurch likened the My Dream Team Builder tool to Amazon's recommender system for products or Netflix's system for movies, she said, "only ours recommends people you might want to form a team with." People who used it provided information about their attributes and their social networks. They also answered questions about the sorts of people they would like on their team. They could specify, for instance, which skills were more important for team members to have and which were less important. They could specify a preference for teammates with significant prior leadership experience or little experience, or they could choose to ignore prior leadership experience entirely. They could specify a preference for people they have enjoyed working with in the past, people who are friends of friends, people who are popular, people who are social brokers—that is, who are connected with numerous groups that are not directly connected to each other—and so on. Considering all the information submitted, the tool compiles a list of recommended teammates, with profiles of each. Users could then choose to click an "Invite" option on the tool to send a pre-scripted e-mail to the potential teammate, inviting him or her to join the team. That person in turn can respond in a variety of ways, including "I'm already on a team, do you want to join mine?" or "Sorry, I have to decline."

Once the teams were formed, DeChurch and her colleagues analyzed how the modalities of assembly affected the assembly mechanisms. They used exponential random graph models, which showed, for example, which people had enjoyed working together in the past and which were now on teams together. After carrying out the analysis, the researchers were able to see how the teams that formed using the builder differed from those that formed using other methods.

The analysis found that teams that had used the builder were more homogeneous in age and also more homogeneous in cultural sensitivity. That was an interesting result, DeChurch noted, "because that's a deep-level characteristic that, if you formed organically, you wouldn't be aware of. But it was attended to by the teams using the builder." On the other hand, the teams using the builder were more heterogeneous by sex. And, not surprisingly, both the teams using the builder and the teams that self-organized without the builder were more likely to contain members who had previously worked together than the teams that were assigned randomly. Thus, although the work is still preliminary, DeChurch sees evidence that the modality of assembly (the four options for degree of control and information) affects assembly mechanisms (the four levels of compositional, person-task fit, relational, or ecosystem considerations) in various ways.

The Effect of Team Assembly Mechanisms on Formation of Team Relationships

In testing whether team assembly mechanisms explained the relationships that formed in the teams, DeChurch and her colleagues modeled those relationships in two different ways. First, they modeled the dependent variable as a typical team-level variable, using sociometric surveys to capture the relationships within the team, asking every person about their relations with every other person, and computing a density score for trust, communication, efficacy, and leadership. In the second approach, they modeled the dependent variable as a dyadic relationship.

In the first approach, a regression analysis showed relationships similar to what had already been seen in the literature (for a review, see Bell, 2007). For Level 1 assembly mechanisms, the main effect was seen for mean extraversion in the group, which was associated with greater trust, communication, and efficacy in the group. There were no significant effects for percent female, mean conscientiousness, mean intercultural sensitivity, or age difference (coefficient of variation). For the Level 3 assembly mechanism (prior relationships), there was a significant effect for leadership but not for trust, communication, or efficacy.

However, when DeChurch analyzed the same variables at the dyadic level using Exponential Random Graph Models, the data revealed much more detail about the characteristics that predicted relationship formation in teams. The analysis allowed her to take into account the traits of the sender in the dyadic relationship, the traits of the receiver, aspects of their relationship, and endogenous structural controls. It also allowed her to jointly consider the unique contribution of each factor (i.e., sender characteristics, receiver characteristics, relational variables, and endogenous controls) in predicting the likelihood that a particular type of tie will form (e.g., a trust tie) while accounting for the influence of all the other factors included in the model.

This analysis, DeChurch reported, showed a number of significant effects. For example, trust ties were more likely to form when the sender—the person doing the trusting—was female. "They are also more likely to form when the receiver—the person you're talking about, do you trust them—is either extroverted or high in conscientiousness. And they are more likely to form if there's a prior relationship." Similarly, leadership ties were more likely to form in teams when there was a prior relationship or when the person being rated as a leader was high in conscientiousness. People were more likely to communicate with those who were high in intercultural sensitivity, and people were more likely to feel they could have an efficacious working relationship with someone who was an extrovert.

The last question DeChurch discussed was whether the way that a team formed changed the relationships that developed within it. "It's essentially the question of, does the dating affect the marriage in teams," she explained. "And it does."

She analyzed how four variables—relational efficacy density, communication density, relational efficacy centralization, and communication centralization—varied according to whether the assembly modality was ad hoc appointment (i.e., random assignment), a blend of assigned and ad hoc self-organized, completely ad hoc self-organized, or data-driven self-organized (see Figure 4-6).

DeChurch's analysis also found that teams whose members all played a role in their organization, either by using the team builder tool or simply by choosing their friends, communicated more and were more confident in their ability to work together effectively than teams with any members who were appointed, even if three of the four team members were self-organized. Furthermore, the teams whose members all played a role in the organization talked more evenly. "So communication is not going through one person, it is going through multiple people, and they are also more balanced in their efficacy," DeChurch said. "So they are not just confident that they can rely on one person, but everyone is confident in the ability to work with everybody else."

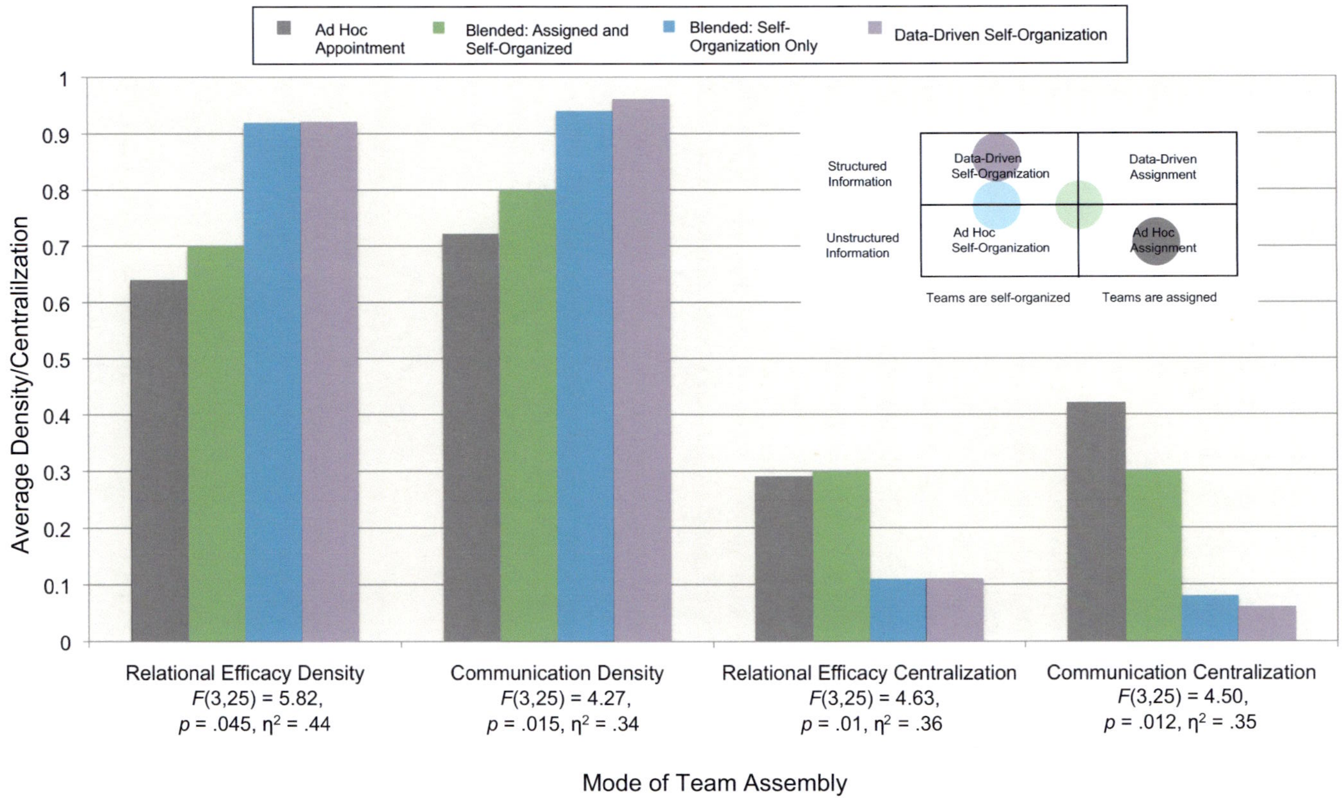

FIGURE 4-6 The effect of team assembly modality on the density and centralization of team communication and efficacy networks.
SOURCE: DeChurch presentation.

Thus, DeChurch summarized, the study offers several intriguing indications of how the team assembly process can affect the team's ultimate performance. "We're seeing evidence that the modalities of how teams assemble are fundamentally changing the information that they are attending to," she said. For example, data-driven self-assembly, as done with the team builder program, allows people to consider deep-level characteristics when choosing team members. "Intercultural sensitivity is something you couldn't know about. So this opens up a lot of interesting possibilities about information that can be considered in advance to make a team more effective that previously would have been unavailable without some sort of infrastructure."

These new possibilities, in turn, suggest three new directions in team staffing and assembly. First, she said, programmatic research on team assembly mechanisms is needed that considers all four of the levels rather than just one. Second, programmatic research examining the consequences of team assembly modalities is needed. "We need to think systematically about how tinkering with the formation of teams comes to impact the nature of the relationships that develop within the teams." Finally, it will be important to take relational analyses seriously. "In organizational behavior we all love to say, 'We have individuals who are nested within teams who are nested within organizations,' but that is not really what teams look like," DeChurch said. "We have individuals, and we have dyads that form patterns of relationships which constitute team-level phenomena." In other words, according to DeChurch, the team-level phenomena emerge from the dyadic relationships, and studies that are more relational in nature may be the key to detect the effects of team assembly on team performance than studies that aggregate everything.

DISCUSSION

The roundtable discussion after the presentations from the panelists on Group Composition Processes and Performance touched on a number of issues related to the understanding and measurement of group-related characteristics.

Military Applications

Invited presenter Paul Sackett (presentation summarized in Chapter 5) started one line of discussion by asking about group-relevant information that might be collected pre-accession. At that point in the military recruitment process, he noted, there is no information about what exactly an individual might be doing or what team he or she might be joining. Later, when jobs are assigned and teams are formed, Sackett said, it will clearly be valuable to have access to information that offers insights into how an individual will perform on a team. So, what information should be collected at the pre-entry stage, he asked, before anything is known about which teams the individual might join?

Gerald Goodwin, of the U.S. Army Research Institute for the Behavioral and Social Sciences (ARI), modified and expanded Sackett's question. "There essentially are three types of decisions that we are considering this information to make," he said. "One is the selection decision: Do you get into the military? One is the classification decision: What occupation or job can you have? And the third is the assignment decision: What unit do you get assigned to, where do you go?" Thus, different types of information will be needed at different times. "What information would you want to get pre-accessioning—which is where we collect most of this information," Goodwin asked, "and what information would you want to get somewhere else, and when and where would you want to get it?"

Woolley replied that social perceptiveness and communication skills are two things that could be measured in the pre-accession phase to increase the likelihood that recruits will perform better on teams. Tannenbaum added that most group-related characteristics appear to be more relevant to assignment than selection. That comment led to a discussion on when these assessments should be made, and Tannenbaum noted that it might make sense to do the assessments in the pre-accession phase, since they do not take too long to complete and would then be available for future assignment decisions. That would only work, however, if the traits were stable over time. Because recruits are often about 18 years old and entering a new phase of their lives, the stability of some of these traits may be an issue. For example, Tannenbaum continued, he does not have the necessary data to say with certainty that TREO scores would be stable. If the evidence indicates that they are not always stable, then it would be necessary to carry out the tests later than pre-accession and closer to the time that soldiers are assigned to their teams.

Following up on that point, Sackett said, "Let's assume [the attribute being measured is] stable, or let's assume we're making an assignment decision shortly enough after accession that you're not worrying about instability. Is there any reason per se to have the information pre-accession, or is it simply needed pre-assignment?" Tannenbaum replied that the main reason to do it pre-accession would be because there is already a testing mechanism in place, and the group-related measures could be jointly administered. On the other hand, he said, given the large numbers of applicants who never enlist or who do not make it through basic training, it might make sense to hold off, if there is some later point at which it is convenient to assess soldiers' group-related characteristics.

DeChurch then offered a reason to administer the tests during pre-accession testing. Because the research indicates that some combinations of team members may be more effective than others, it may make sense to try to have a good distribution of recruits in terms of the different traits they bring to teams. Otherwise, once the soldiers are assigned to teams, it may turn out that there are not enough of some types of team members and too many of others—not enough innovators, say, or too many doers—and some teams will end up with a less than optimum collection of members. So, she said, it might be useful to have a better idea of team factors that should be considered during the selection process.

The assignment phase may benefit the most from assessments of group-related characteristics, Tannenbaum suggested. For example, TREO could prove to be quite useful in assisting assignment decisions, as it allows for multiple variables to be maintained and manipulated simultaneously when considering potential team combinations. DeChurch added that, when assembling groups, she considers it important to know about previous relationships among the potential team members. So she sees value in taking into account the Level 3 (relational) and Level 4 (ecosystem) compositional factors from her model. This would probably not be useful for soldiers during their first assignments, she added, since they will be unlikely to have worked with any of their team members before joining the Army, but it will be an important consideration in later assignments.

Woolley reinforced Tannenbaum's comments by saying that, while the individuals' skills, abilities, and interests are important to take into account when assigning people to a team, what the team members do in combination will be as important, if not more important, than their individual capabilities. "All of the research presented [at the workshop] strongly suggests that there is a combination of capabilities that comes together and influences how the unit performs and that needs to be taken into account in making these assignments," Woolley said. Testing to inform team selection does not have to be administered during the initial screening of recruits, she added, but it will likely be beneficial to conduct in the early stages of a soldier's career.

Adaptability

Paul Gade, a research professor at George Washington University and previously on the ARI staff, introduced the issue of adaptability by describing a study of surgical teams in a shock trauma center (Klein et al., 2006). The study found that the individuals on the team changed their roles, who was in charge, and how the team functioned, depending on what the situation was and who was the best qualified to make decisions in that particular situation. Could such adaptability be included in assessments, he asked, and would it be an individual measure of adaptability or would it be a team measure that was either in place of or in addition to individual adaptability?

DeChurch answered that it is important to think about where team adaptability resides, and she suggested that it can be found more in the processes and the states of teams, rather than in their performance. For example, do the team members understand where the different types of knowledge and skills on the team lie? Knowing that could help predict how well the team members could adapt if they were given a different task or if something in the environment changed. "I think understanding adaptability is really understanding the nature of the interactions in teams and the collective properties," she said.

Building on DeChurch's comment, Woolley noted that her own data linking collective intelligence with learning suggest that collective intelligence probably plays a large role in adaptability as well. "There are various definitions of learning in the literature," she said, "but almost all of them include some level of adaptation when you're talking about it at the group level. So I would say that the same principles that enhance collective intelligence in groups probably also enhance adaptability."

Tannenbaum added that there are probably some individual correlates to adaptability as well. Openness to learning and other personality traits in team members are likely to have at least a small relationship with the adaptability of the team. Still, he said, team adaptability is probably related more to the mix of who happens to be on the team, as well as the culture of the team and the surrounding organization. For example, is it acceptable for someone on the team to step up and say, "I'm not the designated team leader, but I'm going to speak up here"? This is an important factor in the medical world, he said. "The extent to which the attending surgeon sets the stage before an operation has way more to do with whether people are likely to speak up and say, 'Sorry this is the wrong leg you're about to operate on' than [with] individual personality variables. So I think the intervention point there is probably more at the team level."

Tannenbaum added that a related concept is team resilience, which he characterized as referring to how teams respond when they find themselves in difficult situations—and whether they do it in a way that maintains resources and team functionality in addition to just getting through it. "What's interesting about it," he said, "is that at the team level it's different than at the individual level." For instance, a team could be composed of members who are all very individually resilient—they are not likely to succumb to post-traumatic stress disorder—but they may not be great team members, and the team itself does not end up being resilient. So this is another team variable that may be beneficial to consider at the collective level, he concluded.

The Issue of Sufficient Data

Committee member Patrick Kyllonen observed that a fundamental challenge to doing research on teams is collecting sufficient data. It is already difficult to obtain sufficient data to facilitate research on individuals, he said, and the history of intelligence research has had a number of "false alarms" that resulted from sample sizes that were too small. Research on teams requires even more data, Kyllonen continued, in part due to the fact that each team has multiple individuals, but there are other reasons as well. As an example, he noted that DeChurch's claim that research on teams should involve Level 3 and Level 4 observations means that one will need data on individuals' prior relationships with each other and on individuals' prior team memberships.

Kyllonen asked what strategies are available for gathering the large amounts of data that will be necessary for this sort of research. "To get to these higher levels, it's going to require not tens or hundreds, but it's going to require [data on] thousands of people to get anything at all generalizable," he said.

Tannenbaum acknowledged that this is a serious problem. "As the unit of analysis goes up, it's more difficult to gather data." It is harder to gather data at the team level than at the individual level and harder to gather data at the organizational level than at the team level, he said. If the payoffs seem great enough, then it might make sense to carry out "unobtrusive measurements" on Army teams that have already been assembled and are operational, specifically to gather data to use in analyses. But the field is still in its infancy, he suggested, and "at some point there may be some breakthroughs that occur that allow data to be gathered more readily from existing teams that we could use in future research."

DeChurch offered two additional suggestions to facilitate data gathering on teams. One was to use longitudinal research. "I think we have to get beyond the variances between teams and look more meaningfully at modeling the variance within a team over time." Gathering data over time may make it possible to access much more explanatory power than is possible with static measurements. Her second suggestion was to build a community infrastructure and use it to link and share databases. As has been done in other areas of science, rules could be instituted that a paper would not be accepted for publication unless the researchers submitted their data to the central repository so that other researchers could have access to it.

REFERENCES

Aggarwal, I., and A.W. Woolley. (2013). Do you see what I see? The effect of members' cognitive styles on team processes and errors in task execution. *Organizational Behavior and Human Decision Processes*, 122(1):92-99.

Aggarwal, I., A.W. Woolley, C.F. Chabris, and T.W. Malone. (unpublished). Learning How to Coordinate: The Moderating Role of Cognitive Diversity on the Relationship Between Collective Intelligence and Team Learning. Carnegie Mellon University Working Paper. Abstract available: http://works.bepress.com/anita_woolley/1 [July 2013].

Baren-Cohen, S., S. Wheelwright, J. Hill, Y. Raste, and I. Plumb. (2001). The "Reading the Mind in the Eyes Test" revised version: A study with normal adults, and adults with Asperger syndrome or high-functioning autism. *Journal of Child Psychology and Psychiatry*, 42(2):241-251.

Bell, S.T. (2007). Deep-level composition variables as predictors of team performance: A meta-analysis. *Journal of Applied Psychology*, 92(3):595-615.

Bell, S.T., A.J. Villado, M.A. Lukasik, L. Belau, and A.L. Briggs. (2011). Getting specific about demographic diversity variable and team performance relationships: A meta-analysis. *Journal of Management*, 37(3):709-743.

Chen, G.M., and W.J. Starosta. (2000). Intercultural sensitivity. In L.A. Samovar and R.E. Porter (Eds.), *Intercultural Communication: A Reader* (pp. 406-413). Belmont, CA: Wadsworth.

Deary, I.J. (2000). *Looking Down on Human Intelligence: From Psychometrics to the Brain.* New York: Oxford University Press.

Donnellan, M.B., F.L. Oswald, B.M. Baird, and R.E. Lucas. (2006). The mini-IPIP scales: Tiny-yet-effective measures of the Big Five factors of personality. *Psychological Assessment*, 18(2):192-203.

Engel, D., A.W. Woolley, L.X. Jing, C.F. Chabris, and T.W. Malone. (unpublished). Reading the Mind in the Eyes Predicts Collective Intelligence, Even Without Seeing Eyes. Available: https://mitsloan.mit.edu/about/detail.php?in_spseqno=51955 [July 2013].

Guimera, R., B. Uzzi, J. Spiro, and L.A.N. Amaral. (2005). Team assembly mechanisms determine collaboration network structure and team performance. *Science*, 308(5722):697-702.

Keegan, B., D. Gergle, and N. Contractor. (2012). Do editors or articles drive collaboration? Multilevel statistical network analysis of Wikipedia coauthorship. In S. Poltrack and C. Simone (Eds.), *Proceedings of the 2012 ACM Conference on Computer-Supported Cooperative Work (CSCW)* (pp. 427-436). New York: Association for Computing Machinery. Available: http://dl.acm.org/citation.cfm?doid=2145204.2145271 [July 2013].

Klein, K.J., C.J. Ziegert, A.P. Knight, and Y. Xiao. (2006). Dynamic delegation: Shared, hierarchical and deindividualized leadership in extreme action teams. *Administrative Science Quarterly*, 50(4):590-621.

Lungeanu, A., N.S. Contractor, D. Carter, and L.A. DeChurch. (2013). A hypergraph approach to understanding the assembly of scientific research teams. In D. Carter (Chair), *Teams on the Hyper-Edge: Using Hypergraph Network Methodology to Understand Teams.* Symposium conducted at the Interdisciplinary Network for Group Research Conference, July, Atlanta, GA. Presentation information available: https://www.conftool.net/ingroup2013/index.php?page=browseSessions&form_session=3&CTSID_INGROUP2013=RHaHuEd1CuQISf6V3MS6t85TnJ1 [July 2013].

Mathieu, J.E., S.I. Tannenbaum, J.S. Donsbach, and G.M. Alliger. (2013). Achieving optimal team composition for success. In E. Salas, S.I. Tannenbaum, D. Cohen, and G. Latham (Eds.), *Developing and Enhancing Teamwork in Organizations: Evidence-based Best Practices and Guidelines* (pp. 520-551). San Francisco, CA: Jossey-Bass.

Mathieu, J.E., S.I. Tannenbaum, M.R. Kukenburger, J.S. Donsbach, and G.M. Alliger. (unpublished). Team Role Experiences and Orientations: The Development of a Measure of Tests of Nomological Network Relations. Available: http://admin.business.uconn.edu/PortalVBVS/DesktopModules/Staff/staff.aspx?&uid=jmathieu [July 2013].

Myaskovsky, L., E. Unikel, and M.A. Dew. (2005). Effects of gender diversity on performance and interpersonal behavior in small work groups. *Sex Roles*, 52(9):645-657.

Spearman, C. (1904). "General intelligence" objectively determined and measured. *American Journal of Psychology*, 15(2):201-292.

Stewart, G.L. (2006). A meta-analytic review of relationships between team design features and team performance. *Journal of Management*, 32(1):29-55.

Tannenbaum, S.I., J.S. Donsbach, G.M. Alliger, J.E. Mathieu, K.A. Metcalf, and G.F. Goodwin. (2010). *Forming Effective Teams: Testing the Team Composition System (TCS) Algorithms and Decision Aid.* Paper presented at the 27th Annual Army Science Conference, Orlando, FL. Available: http://www.groupoe.com/groupoe-company/team/97-scott-tannenbaum.html [July 2013].

Woolley, A.W., C.F. Chabris, A. Pentland, N. Hashmi, and T.W. Malone. (2010). Evidence for a collective intelligence factor in the performance of human groups. *Science*, 330(6004):686-688.

5

New Approaches and Capabilities in Assessment

In addition to changing and adding to *what* is measured, as was described in previous chapters, assessments can also be improved by changing *how* traits are measured. Although the Army already employs a well-developed battery of tests, recent and impending advances in assessment methods offer the potential to improve that testing by improving the accuracy of a test, by providing assessments of traits that have not previously been tested (including team-related traits), or by making the tests easier—and thus faster—to administer, making it possible to include additional assessments in the time available.

Many of the workshop participants, speaking generally, noted that many emerging assessment measures tend to focus on more complex tasks, to use simulations more extensively, and to put greater emphasis on more realistic and real-time tasks. These new assessments also gather more data and more types of data, including timing data and longitudinal data, which in turn increases the types of analyses that can be performed.

Two speakers in particular discussed such new approaches and capabilities in assessment. Paul Sackett, who spoke during a panel on the second day, categorized the various approaches to improve assessment and gave a broad overview of current thinking on the subject. The workshop's keynote speaker, Alina von Davier, discussed current and potential future research at the Educational Testing Service relevant to the next generation of assessments.

A TAXONOMY FOR WAYS TO IMPROVE SELECTION SYSTEMS

Over time, researchers and assessment experts have suggested a large number of ways to improve assessments. To help organize and make sense of the multitude of suggestions, Paul Sackett, a distinguished professor of psychology and liberal arts at the University of Minnesota in Minneapolis, offered a taxonomy for thinking about ways to improve the quality of selection systems. In his presentation, he also offered a number of specific examples of approaches to improving assessments.

In particular, Sackett drew from a review article he published with a colleague in 2008, which proposed four categories of methods to improve selection systems: (1) identify new predictor constructs, (2) measure existing predictor constructs better, (3) develop a better understanding of the criterion domain, and (4) improve the specification and estimation of predictor–criterion relationships (Sackett and Lievens, 2008). A number of the presentations in the workshop, he noted, had already focused on new predictor constructs—for example, working memory capacity, inhibitory control, and personal agency—so Sackett focused his presentation on the other three categories.

Improving Measurements of Existing Predictor Constructs

In addition to identifying new predictor constructs, another way to improve assessments would be to measure existing predictor constructs better. "We need to think systematically about that," Sackett said. To encourage the workshop participants to think about how one might begin to improve existing predictor constructs, he offered three specific examples: contextualized personality items, narrower dimensions of personality measures, and use of real-time faking warnings.

Contextualized Personality Items

To begin, Sackett addressed personality assessments. Many personality inventories simply do not provide context, he said. The questions are overly generalized, such as, "Agree or disagree: I like keeping busy."

But there has been a great deal of work in the area of industrial and organization psychology, Sackett noted, that indicates adding context can greatly improve the predictive ability of assessments (Shaffer and Postlethwaite, 2012). "Just add two words," he said, "At the end of that item, add 'at work': 'I like keeping busy *at work*.' We're not talking fancy contextualization to a specific job, but very, very generic contextualizations."

Sackett described the results of a meta-analysis that examined the effect of adding context to assessment items. In particular, the analysis compared standard personality assessment items with contextualized items—that is, items that had been modified by asking about behavior at work rather than behavior in general. The two types of assessments were compared with supervisory ratings of job performance to determine their correlation with those ratings. The contextualized measures, Sackett reported, reflect the supervisory ratings more accurately. For conscientiousness, for example, the validity of the contextualized measure was 0.30 versus 0.22 for the standard measure. For emotional stability it was 0.17 versus 0.12, for extraversion it was 0.25 versus 0.08, and for openness it was 0.19 versus 0.02. The average validity for the contextualized measures was 0.24 versus 0.11 for the standard measures (Shaffer and Postlethwaite, 2012). Sackett noted that adding context thus doubled the validity of the measures.

Narrower Dimensions of Personality Measures

A variety of researchers have discussed the idea of dividing the Big Five personality traits into smaller, more focused traits. In 2007, for example, DeYoung and colleagues suggested splitting each of the Big Five traits into two:

- neuroticism [emotional stability] becomes volatility and withdrawal,
- agreeableness becomes compassion and politeness,
- conscientiousness becomes industriousness and orderliness,
- extraversion becomes enthusiasm and assertiveness, and
- openness to experience becomes intellect and openness.

Intuitively the divisions make sense, Sackett said, and there is also some evidence that the way the splits are made is not arbitrary. In particular, he described one study that indicated that such splits may be useful in terms of their predictive power.

In 2006, Dudley and colleagues carried out a meta-analysis of how well global measures of conscientiousness predict task performance versus the predictive power of four conscientious facets: achievement, dependability, order, and cautiousness. Industrial and organizational psychologists generally accept that, among the various measures of personality, conscientiousness is the best predictor of task performance, Sackett noted. The meta-analysis found that the validity of conscientiousness as a predictor of task performance—that is, how well it predicted performance—was driven mainly by the achievement and dependability facets of conscientiousness. The facets of order and cautiosness did not contribute, according to Sackett. "So to the extent that you spend half of your items trying to cover the full range [of conscientiousness], you're including stuff that, at least for prediction in work settings, doesn't carry any freight," Sackett said. "It's not useful."

Furthermore, the two facets predicted different aspects of work success. "The achievement piece receives the dominant weight if you're predicting task performance, while dependability receives the dominant weight in predicting job dedication and the avoidance of counterproductive work behaviors," he said. This sort of nuanced approach to testing could be valuable in pre-employment assessments.

Use of Real-Time Faking Warnings

In personality assessments, there is always concern that people will attempt to manipulate impressions to convey themselves more favorably than reality. This, of course, produces less valid test results.

One approach to dealing with this problem is to use responses to early items in order to assess faking and then intervene with a warning to those who appear to be skewing their answers. "You've got to word [the warning] really carefully," Sackett cautioned, to avoid making accusations about lying or cheating. "You say, this is a pattern that is typical of people who are trying to improve their performance; we're going to take you back to the top and encourage you to respond honestly."

One study in which Sackett was involved looked for "blatant extreme responding," something that generally appears in only a small percentage of test takers. After one-third of the items had been administered in a test given to managerial candidates, a warning was issued to those who were exhibiting this blatant extreme responding. The rate of extreme responding was halved—from 6 percent to only 3 percent—after the warning (Landers et al., 2011).

A second study involved an assessment for administrative jobs in China (Fan et al., 2012). A number of socially desirable items were included relatively early in the test, and a warning was given to those people who were exceeding a certain threshold.

The result, as shown in Figure 5-1, demonstrates that those with low impression-management scores continued to obtain low scores as the assessment progressed. But those with high impression-management scores produced markedly lower scores after receiving the online warning.

Better Understanding of the Criterion Domain

Another way to improve assessments is to develop a better understanding of the criterion domain. Sackett offered two examples of this approach: predictor–criterion matching and identification of new criteria.

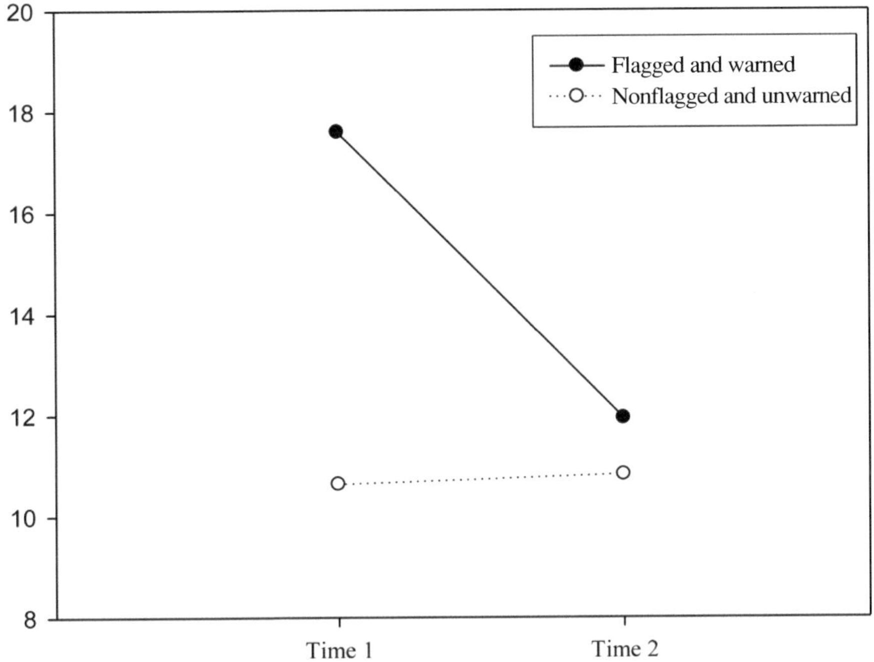

FIGURE 5-1 The effect of real-time faking warnings.
SOURCE: Fan et al. (2012).

Predictor–Criterion Matching

People tend to wonder whether test X or construct X is a good predictor, Sackett said, but that begs the additional question: A good predictor of what? In particular, there is a tendency to think about "performance" as a single thing and thus to ask whether a test is a good predictor of performance. The industrial and organizational psychology literature, he said, is full of this sort of thing. For example, it is common to claim that general cognitive ability is the best predictor of job performance, he added, but that really depends on what facet of job performance one cares about.

As an example, Sackett showed some results from the classic Project A study by the U.S. Army (McHenry et al., 1990). Table 5-1 shows validity scores for three measures—general cognitive ability, need for achievement, and dependability—and three performance domains—task performance, citizenship, and counterproductive work behavior. (The latter are labels applied to the performance domains by Sackett, not by the original researchers.) Task performance is simply how well a person completes assigned tasks, Sackett said. Citizenship measures such things as con-

TABLE 5-1 Validity Scores for Three Measures (Predictors) and Three Performance Domains (Criteria)

	Predictors		
Criteria	General Cognitive Ability	Need for Achievement	Dependability
Task Performance	.43	.11	.11
Citizenship	.22	.30	.22
Counterproductive Work Behavior	.11	.18	.30

SOURCE: Sackett presentation.

tributing extra effort, helping others, and supporting the organization. Counterproductive behavior is self-explanatory. (In Table 5-1, the validity scores for counterproductive work behavior are reverse-coded so that the direction of the correlations remains the same for all three domains.)

"Is general cognitive ability the best predictor? Yes, it's the best predictor of task performance. It beats need for achievement and dependability." Sackett added that it is clearly not the best predictor of citizenship or counterproductive work behavior. So it is important to think carefully about what one is trying to predict, he concluded, because using the wrong criterion in correlation computations may nullify the results.

As another example, Sackett described a study of a situational judgment test used for medical school admissions in Belgium. A subject is shown a video of a doctor interacting with a patient, the video is stopped, and the subject is asked what should be done next. It is a way of testing a subject's interpersonal skills more than anything else. It was found that this situational judgment test had predictive power in medical schools that had a "whole person" focus but not in those schools that took a "scientific" focus. Similarly, the test predicted performance in internships and in rotations but not in academic courses (Lievens et al., 2005).

"If you think about it," Sackett said, "that's what it should do. But if you don't think straight, and you just grab the overall GPA [grade point average] as a criterion measure, you'll reach a very different conclusion as to whether this test has any value." Thus, it is important to think carefully about what a test is being used to predict and what makes sense, conceptually, for a test to predict.

Identification of New Criteria

Sackett's second approach to better understanding of criterion domains is to identify new criteria. For example, Pulakos and colleagues (2000) developed the notion of adaptive performance at work, developed measures of it, and then examined predictors of it. This approach has become quite popular recently, Sackett said. Employers are saying things like, "The world is changing. I want people who can quickly change. What can we do?" Sackett noted that a similar strategy could be applied to many other domains, and he suggested two in particular: teamwork performance and crisis performance.

There are two different strategies for dealing with new factors like this, Sackett said. One is to develop methods to measure factors directly in job applicants—to put people in simulations where things change and observe if they can adapt or to assess their teamwork skills. In this case, the new construct is put on the predictor side, where adaptability or some other new construct is used as a predictor of performance.

Sometimes, though, it may not be feasible to develop or conduct the necessary assessments to use the construct as a predictor prior to employment. In that case, Sackett suggested that the construct can be used as a criterion instead. Once someone is working in the job, measures can be developed to assess how well he or she adapts to change or deals with teamwork, and then one looks for predictors that can be used to predict these new measures of performance.

Improved Understanding of Predictor–Criterion Relationships

According to Sackett, the final route to better assessment systems is to improve one's specification and estimation of predictor–criterion relationships. He offered three specific examples: profiles of predictors, interactive relationships, and nonlinear relationships.

Profiles of Predictors

A set of predictors, such as the Big Five personality traits, can be thought of as a collection of numerical values, Sackett suggested, and one can then ask, what about that set of predictors is most predictive of a certain criterion? In 2002, Davison and Davenport developed a technique that focuses explicitly on criterion-related profiles. This approach separates the variance attributable to the *level* (or mean elevation) of the predictors and the *profile* (or deviations from the mean) of the predictors.

The difference can be seen by looking at the two graphs in Figure 5-2, each of which shows the Big Five personality trait profiles of two people. The two people in the graph on the left have profiles that are radically different, but they have the same mean level, if one thinks of the profile in terms of a composite value, where a high score on one attribute compensates for a low score on the other. By contrast, the two people in the graph on the right clearly differ substantially in level but are identical in profile. "The conceptual question is, where does the predictive power

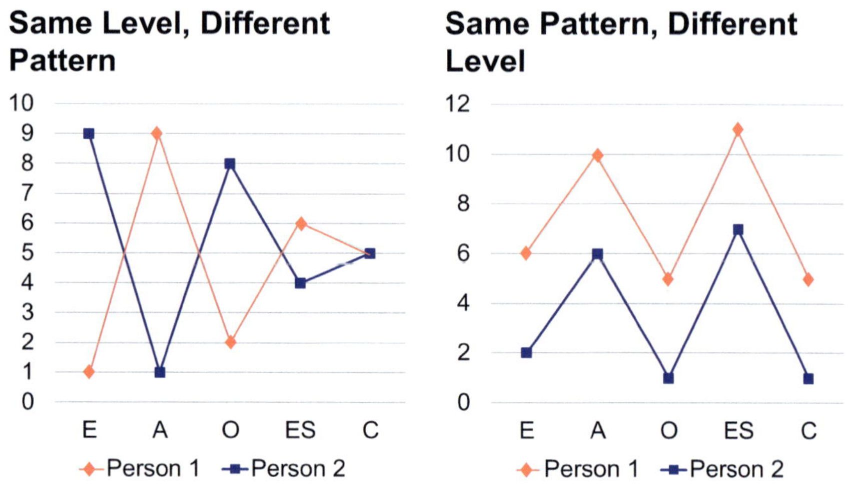

FIGURE 5-2 Variance in level of personality measures (right) versus variance in personality profile (left): A notional example.
NOTE: A = agreeableness; C = conscientiousness; E = extraversion; ES = emotional stability; O = openness.
SOURCE: Reprinted with permission from Shen and Sackett (2010).

come from?" Sackett asked. "Does the predictive power come from level, or does the predictive power come from profile?"

When Sackett and his colleague examined how the Big Five personality traits predicted citizenship and counterproductive behavior in a group of 900 university employees, they found that the predictive power for citizenship came completely from the profile level. For counterproductive behavior, however, both the level and the pattern were important predictors (Shen and Sackett, 2012). "I want to suggest that we think about things like this," he said.

Interactive Relationships

Sackett's second example of improving predictor–criterion relationships involved interactive relationships among traits. It is a truism in work psychology, Sackett said, that performance is a function of ability times motivation. "You can have all the ability in the world, but if motivation is zero, nothing is going to happen. You can have all the motivation in the world, and if ability is zero, nothing's going to happen."

While most psychologists study the independent contributions of ability and motivational traits, Sackett suggested that perhaps they should be looking at their interactions. The published findings in this area are a mixed bag, he said. Some studies find some evidence of interactive relationships, some do not (for a review, see Sackett et al., 1998). But he suggested it is important to think clearly about the issue and to examine the possibility of predictors working together interactively.

Nonlinear Relationships

As his third example, Sackett suggested that it may be worth considering the possibility of nonlinear relationships between predictors and criteria. Psychologists usually model predictor–criterion relationships as linear, and there is good support for this in the ability domain, he said. However, it seems to be a questionable assumption in other domains.

To illustrate, Sackett described a dissertation in development by one of his students. Using raw data on 117 samples of Big Five personality trait performance relationships, the student is examining the relationships between the personality traits and various criteria, such as job performance. One example is the relationship between conscientiousness and an overall job performance measure.

More conscientiousness is better up to a point, but at some point conscientiousness leads to rigidity, and more of it is not better for job performance. Thus modeling the relationship of conscientiousness with performance as linear may misrepresent reality.

The data show something similar for sociability versus overall job performance. Again, more sociability is better until it is not. At some point, being more sociable starts to hurt job performance. However, when the data are analyzed more carefully, Sackett cautioned, there is more to it than may first appear. By coding which types of jobs require a great deal of interaction with other people and then looking separately at jobs with high interaction and low interaction, Sackett's student uncovered a significantly different picture. For those jobs where interacting with other people is a key part of the job, he found that more sociability is always a good thing, and there is never a point where the graph turns downward. By contrast, for jobs in which personal interaction is not a key component, too much sociability is very clearly a bad thing, and the graph turns down sharply after a certain point.

The bottom line, Sackett concluded, is that it pays to look more closely at predictor–criterion relationships and to not be too quick to assume that a simple linear relationship accurately describes reality.

PSYCHOMETRICS FOR A NEW GENERATION OF ASSESSMENTS

In the workshop's keynote address, Alina von Davier, a research director at the Educational Testing Service (ETS) and leader of the company's Center for Advanced Psychometrics, provided an overview of the coming generation of assessments and then discussed in detail one particular area of research, exploring the use of collaborative problem-solving tasks to assess cognitive skills, under way at ETS.

A Taxonomy of the New Generation of Assessments

One of the factors driving the development of new assessments, von Davier observed, is the change in how people learn and work. For example, education is being redefined by complex computer–human interactions, intelligent tutorials, educational games, adaptive feedback, and other technology-driven innovations, but educational assessments have not kept up with these changes. "We [ETS] are the largest testing organization," she said, "and we have to think about how we can bridge this void between educational practice and educational assessment." To do so, she said, test makers will need to understand how to use the advances in technology, statistics, data mining, and the learning sciences to support the creation of a new generation of assessments. ETS has just begun to investigate the psychometric challenges associated with these types of assessments. It has also been looking into ways of collaborating with colleagues from other fields, such as artificial intelligence, cognitive sciences, engineering, physics, and statistics.

von Davier then discussed the various ways in which new and coming assessments differ from previous assessments, organized into a number of categories.

The first category was assessments that represent new types of applications. There are, for instance, assessments of skills that have not commonly been assessed in the past, such as group problem solving. There is also a greater interest in assessments that provide diagnostic and actionable information and a greater emphasis on noncognitive measures. Furthermore, there are assessments aimed at different age groups, such as younger children.

Many new types of assessment tasks are also being developed. Some of the most interesting assessments in this second category, von Davier said, use various complex tasks, such as simulations and collaborative tasks. People are working on using serious games as a context for the assessment and, eventually, as an unobtrusive way to test. And there is research on the iterative development of tasks, where the task itself is developed over time to match the test-taker's ability.

A third category is new modes of assessment administration. Among these are continuous testing and distributed testing, both of which are already in use. ETS now has tests that are administered in an almost continuous mode, she said. "They bring with them interesting challenges, from the measurement point of view, from the development-of-items point of view, and from the statistical analysis point of view." Distributed testing, she explained, refers to a formative type of assessment in which different tests are administered over a period of time. Another mode of administration being explored is the observational rating of real-time performances. And the future will also see a greater use of both technology and interactivity, she suggested.

A fourth way in which new assessments differ from existing ones is in the stakes of assessment. Many of the new assessments are being applied differently in society, she said. More and more often people are taking into account economic issues in test-driven decision making. For example, is it more cost-effective to use tests to improve selection or to spend less on tests and more on training? This sort of economics-driven decision will become increasingly common in the future, von Davier predicted.

Finally, von Davier said, the new generation of assessments will differ from the previous generation in the type of data they produce, both their process data and their outcome data. In the past, for example, tests measured results from one point in time (providing discrete data), but in the future, von Davier believes, more and more tests will be longitudinal in nature (providing continuous data). Thus, the data will have a time element. She imagines tests in the future that will produce data from frequent or continuous test paradigms. There will be outcome data from complex tasks, simulations, and collaborations, all of which will produce very different types of data than tests based on classic item response theory, she explained.

Perhaps even more challenging will be the process data that are collected: detailed information about the processes that the students went through as they carried out their complex tasks, simulations, and collaborations. There will be such things as timing data and eye tracking data.

What will be quite interesting from a statistical point of view, von Davier said, is that there will be an increased mixture of continuous and discrete data. For example, ETS has started to use automatic scoring engines, which can generate continuous scores. In the past, test scores have generally been discrete. "We will need to handle both types of data, continuous and discrete, in the future," she said.

These new types of assessments will require consideration of how to fulfill traditional assessment requirements such as reliability, validity, and comparability. In particular, von Davier listed the following issues:

- What does it mean to have a reliable test that contains complex tasks? How can we define and elicit the right evidence from the process data?

- How long should a task be so that the process data are rich enough to allow for the intensive and dependent longitudinal models?
- How many tasks are needed for a reliable assessment?
- What is the best way to evaluate the validity of an assessment? What type of data should be collected for a predictive type of study?
- How can one construct complex problems that differ from one administration to the next but that are still comparable? In other words, how can we rethink the notion of test equating?

Assessing Cognitive Skills Through Collaborative Problem-Solving Tasks

The new Center for Advanced Psychometrics at ETS, which officially started on January 1, 2013, under von Davier's leadership, is intended to focus on this next generation of assessments through research and development projects, she explained. To begin, it will investigate new types of tasks, simulations, and game-based assessments. To illustrate the sorts of new assessments that are coming—and the challenges that they pose—von Davier described one particular research direction that has begun at the new center.

At ETS, von Davier and her group are exploring how to use collaborative problem-solving tasks to assess cognitive skills. The research ideas discussed in her workshop address are also discussed in a recent paper (von Davier and Halpin, in press). A valid assessment reflects the way people learn and use the skills that are being assessed, she said, but traditional assessments have generally ignored the fact that much learning and work today is done in collaboration. Collaborative problem-solving tasks are intended to capture this aspect of learning and work.

One question she faced in working on such tasks was how to define success in this context. Among the several possibilities, she noted, is that success could be defined as a group of individuals performing better than each individual alone. Or it could be defined as the group performing a task faster than the individuals could do it alone. In her work, she said, she has used the former definition of a successful collaboration.

With a diagram, von Davier sketched out a framework for how one might assess cognitive skills using collaborative problem-solving tasks (see Figure 5-3).

The traditional assessments are indicated on the right-hand side of the figure. "That is what we are doing right now," she said. "We have a particular skill, where we try to measure both knowledge and problem-solving in isolation." These are assessed using multiple-choice, open-ended, and portfolio tasks. To advance assessment, von Davier's idea is to add a collaborative task that measures the same skill (e.g., science)

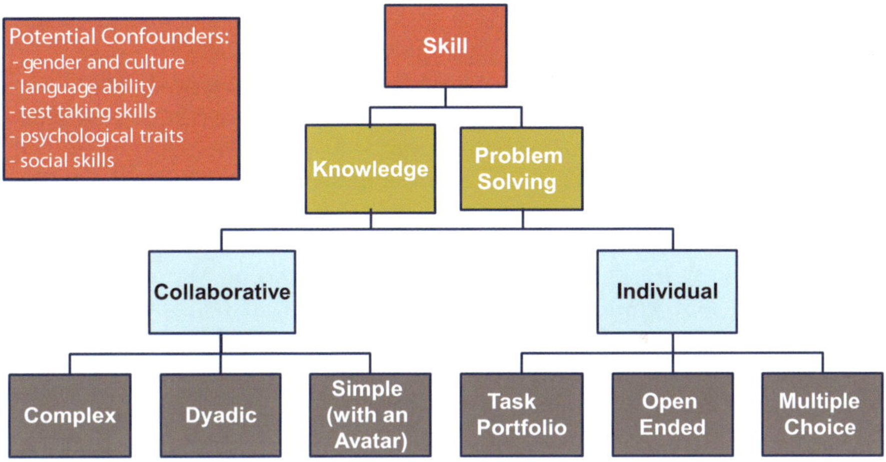

FIGURE 5-3 A framework for assessing cognitive skills with collaborative problem solving.
SOURCE: Reprinted with permission from von Davier and Halpin (in press).

but in a way that is more reflective of how people typically learn and work today. von Davier said that her group is considering several types of tasks to carry out such assessments: simple tasks using an avatar in place of another person, dyadic tasks with two members on a team, and complex tasks that are carried out in a multiuser environment similar to what is used in commercial games. "The question is, how do you elicit the information you need for the measurement from those tasks? We are not quite there yet."

The tests in development will be used to measure cognitive skills only, von Davier said, and other skills—communication skills, collaboration skills, and so on—will be considered as potential confounders. That does not mean that these potential confounders are not important, she added; it simply means that she has chosen, at this stage, not to include them in the measurement model. "It is one way to build an assessment. I am not claiming that this is the best way, but I believe that this is something I know how to do. I think that matters, given that we don't have anything except the use of process data for the measurement of skills."

Data and Scores

A collaborative problem-solving assessment can produce both process and outcome data, von Davier noted. The process data offer an insight into the interaction dynamics of the team members, which is important both for defining collaborative tasks and for evaluating the results of the collaboration.

Previous research has suggested both that people behave differently when they interact in teams than when they work alone and that team members' individual domain scores might not correlate highly with the team's outcome. The latter is a very interesting hypothesis, von Davier said, and one that could be investigated closely using the framework for the assessment mapped out in Figure 5-3. By assessing the differences between the individual problem solving and collaborative problem solving, she said, one could generalize several scores instead of the single total test score that is usual. "In this situation," she said, "we might have a score obtained in isolation, a score obtained in collaboration, and the team score."

Interdependence and Dynamics

In a collaborative problem-solving assessment, von Davier observed, the interactions will change over time and will involve time-lagged interrelationships. Thus, supposing there are two people on a team, the actions of one of them will depend both on the actions of the other and on his or her own past actions. To be beneficial, the statistical models used should accurately describe the dynamics of the interactions.

von Davier believes that the dynamics, which are defined by the interdependence between the individuals on the team, could offer information that could be used to build a hypothesis about the strategy of the team. For example, by analyzing the covariance of the observed variables (the events), one might hypothesize that an unknown variable, such as the team's strategy type, explains why the team chose a particular response and avoided the alternative.

Modeling Strategies for the Process Data

There are a number of modeling strategies available to use on the process data, von Davier said. Few of them come from educational assessment, however, so they must be adapted from other fields. The modeling strategies include dynamic factor analysis, multilevel modeling, dynamic linear models, differential equation models, nonparametric exploratory models such as social networks analysis, intravariability models, hidden Markov models and Bayes nets, machine learning methods, latent class analysis and neural networks, and point processes—which are stochastic processes for discrete events. The last of these strategies is what von Davier is using now.

Modeling Strategies for the Outcome Data

There are three categories of outcome data that are produced by an assessment of collaborative problem-solving tasks: data on individual performance, data on group performance, and data on the contribution of each individual to the group performance. It is well known how to deal with the first, von Davier noted, and there are straightforward ways of dealing with the second as well, simply by assessing, for instance, whether the group solved the problem or not. But dealing with the third type of outcome data is a challenge. "That is a work in progress," she said. "We are trying to integrate the stochastic processes modeling approach with the outcome data approach."

Among the models they are considering applying to outcome data are what von Davier referred to as item response theory–based models. She explained that she meant models that use the same type of rationale that is used in response patterns. Another possibility is using student/learner models from intelligent tutoring systems: "I am open to suggestions from anyone who might have other ideas," she offered.

The Hawkes Process

To analyze the data from collaborative problem-solving tasks, one of the approaches that von Davier and her colleague Peter F. Halpin from New York University are considering is the Hawkes process, which is a stochastic process (including random variables) for discrete events that can easily be extended to a multivariate scenario such as multiple team members.

The idea behind the Hawkes process is that each event stream is a mixture of three different event types. There are spontaneous events, which do not depend on previous events. "Some member of the team just out of the blue has an idea and puts it on the table." Then there are self-responses, which are events that depend on their own past. Perhaps, for instance, one individual has several versions of the same idea. But the third event type is the one that really interests von Davier's team, she said. She described it as "other responses" [responses to others]—events that depend on another person-event stream's past. This is where the modeling of the interactions between two individuals or between the team and an individual takes place.

The Hawkes process, she explained, estimates which events are most likely to belong to each of these three types, based on a temporal structure of the data, that is, based on event times (Halpin and De Boeck, 2013). "We have time-stamped events: Person X said this, person Y said that. This goes on for the entire half an hour of the collaborative problem-solving task. We have the time, and we have the event itself." Von Davier added that her team is now working on using the Hawkes process to analyze the data from collaborative problem-solving tasks.

Possible Approaches for Outcome Data

In the final part of her address to the workshop, von Davier said that she is seeking ways to integrate the models for process data with the outcome data. One idea her team is developing goes further with the Hawkes processes to assign an assessment of correct or incorrect outcome to each event. In other words, they are trying to build what is called a "marked Hawkes Process," where a "mark" is a random variable that describes the information about each event or interaction (such as noting whether the outcome was correct or incorrect). "Then we can incorporate it [the assigned mark] into the Hawkes process that describes the interactions." This work is still in development, she said, and while her team has already obtained promising results, it needs to be applied to expanded datasets.

von Davier's team is also looking at an extension of item response models. The idea is to condition the probability of a successful response from a person not just on the ability of the person, as is traditionally done in item response theory, but also on the response patterns from all the group members. "That is where the challenge comes in," she said. "How can you take into account the sequence of response patterns over time?"

In the future, von Davier indicated, scientists from her center will pursue research in several other directions as well. They will study the best way to model process data from interactive tasks and from complex tasks administered in isolation, such as simulations and educational games. They will also investigate ways of maintaining task comparability and ensuring the fairness of a complex assessment over time. Some of the research projects will target other challenges of the new assessments she listed in her taxonomy.

DISCUSSION

In the discussion following von Davier's keynote address, there was an extensive back-and-forth conversation about outcome criteria and how to code those criteria. Committee member Patrick Kyllonen began by describing a dataset at the National Board of Medical Examiners that contains medical challenges in which physicians are faced with a set of symptoms and then asked to make a judgment or decision. It is interactive, with the physician following a virtual case is which he or she is presented with the relevant information and then, at various points, asked to make a decision about what to do next.

The physicians' performance is judged in two different ways. One approach simply looks at the outcome: Did the physician make the correct diagnosis or not? In the second approach, experts go through the process data and make a judgment about each decision. An analogy would be playing a chess game in which experts evaluated every move on whether it was a good move or a bad move. "It is a real data mining approach versus a more theoretical approach," Kyllonen explained.

In other realms, he observed, data mining approaches have generally proven to be stronger, and they have tended to win out over the more theoretical approaches. He then asked von Davier which of the approaches might be more fruitful for coding the results of the collaborative problem-solving tasks. Would it be the data mining approaches, which have beat out the expert judgment approaches in fields from Google's Internet searches to playing chess, or would it be the more evaluative, theoretical approach?

Google's data mining efforts are so successful, von Davier pointed out, because there is so much data to mine. "How many collaborative problem-solving tasks can we put in an assessment? . . . If I can put in only one, and if that will go for 30 minutes, then probably the chain in my process data would be maybe 100, if I am lucky." Thus the data mining would probably not tell her much about that particular situation, and the expert judgment approach would be more useful. "However, if I am able to obtain data, if I can get multiple teams, and if I can get sufficient data to test them, then the answer is positive. I think data mining will have a strong impact on what we do."

In reality, she continued, she is looking for a combination of the two approaches for two reasons. First, she is unlikely to access sufficient data for the procedures to be stable. And, second, "We always like theories. What we will probably be using the data mining for would be to help us construct our theories and replace the expert knowledge."

James Jackson, a member of the National Research Council's Board on Behavioral, Cognitive, and Sensory Sciences, noted that, in general, some tasks differ in whether there is a successful outcome or not and some tasks differ according to their degree of elegance. In a programming task, for example, it is not simply whether one creates a program to do what it needs to do; the issue of elegance also plays a role. This quality of elegance, he suggested, might provide more variation with which to understand how well people are performing a task.

von Davier agreed, adding that this is very close to something her team is trying to do. "There are examples when, say, a very good sports team loses a game. At the end of the game, everybody would say, they played beautifully, and they still lost." What she hopes to be able to do with the Hawkes model is to capture that beautiful interaction. "I think that is where the Hawkes models actually can help because of the way they classify the type of interactions" she continued. For example, one team might have solved the problem and also worked really well together, and the process data along the way would show that. Then there might be another team that also solved the problem, but each of its two members referred only to their own past proposals or ideas during their problem-solving sessions. "That will be an example of a successful solving of the problem, but we will have evidence that the collaboration was not working as well."

Invited presenter James Rounds noted that there is an area of psychotherapy research on process models in which they do similar coding. One of the reasons why there is not more research in the field, he said, is that it costs a lot of money to do the coding. Todd Little, a presenter from the workshop's first panel, suggested one way to address the challenge of coding is to plan for missing data. For more information on Little's ideas

BOX 5-1
Missing Data

In his presentation during the workshop's first panel, Todd Little of the University of Kansas in Lawrence, mentioned the value of missing data techniques in various types of analyses, although he did not go into detail at that point. Later, at various points during the two-day workshop, Little and other attendees offered more detailed suggestions for how missing data techniques could be put to work in research and assessment.

Missing data techniques are ways to deal with data that are missing from a study (for reviews, see Enders, 2010; Graham, 2012; van Buuren, 2012). The data can be missing for various reasons, such as survey participants may choose not to answer certain questions or members of a group chosen to participate in a study may fail to take part altogether. Researchers have developed a number of ways to deal with missing data, such as inserting questions into a survey that are designed to characterize those subjects who fail to answer particular questions—out of discomfort with the subject of a question, for example—and thus allow the imputation of plausible answers to passed-over questions that would yield unbiased estimates of the parameters of any statistical model fit to the post-imputation dataset.

Following James Rounds' presentation, "Rethinking Interests," Little commented that missing data techniques could have been useful in a longitudinal study that Rounds described. A number of participants had dropped out over time, Rounds noted, and Little commented that it was "probably a selective drop-out process." That is, some types of participants were more likely to drop out than others. Little explained that one of the benefits of "modern approaches for treating missing data is that we can, through some clever work, get auxiliary variables into [an] analysis model that would be predictive of that selective process." Then, having characterized which subjects were likely to drop out, it would be possible to use the full-information maximum likelihood estimation—or some other modern missing data technique about the utility of missing data, see Box 5-1, which summarizes several potential applications in research and assessment.

Committee member Georgia Chao said she is facing similar coding challenges in research she is doing with emergency medical teams. Not only is it necessary to have subject matter experts who know about team processes and can code what is going on in the teams but it is also necessary to have subject matter experts in medicine who code the performance of the team.

"It is not always as simple as, 'Does the patient live, or does the patient die?' We [reviewed cases and] were surprised when the medical people said, 'Oh, this is a great case.' We looked and said, 'But the patient died.' They said, 'Yes, but they did everything correctly. They diagnosed it correctly, they gave the right kinds of drugs.' Patients die for all kinds of reasons, so that doesn't drive the success or failure of an event." Coding

such as multiple imputation—to see what the survey response would have looked like without the missing data.

Little referred to another way to use missing data techniques as a "planned missing data design," in which different questions are omitted from different participants' surveys in a carefully structured way—thus creating missing data—and then modern missing data techniques are used to reconstruct the survey as if every subject had answered every question.

One potential application in research might examine whether new constructs provided incremental validity to established constructs, Little suggested. "It would be a very easy thing to create a multiformed, planned missing data design," he said. Different individuals would be tested on different constructs, he explained, and one could have a set of variables that could be used to examine all constructs in one big multivariate model, to see if incremental validity is obtained from any of the constructs, above and beyond what is already being measured.

Little also suggested that planned missing data designs could help in studies such as those described by Alina von Davier that collect a great deal of intensive data through the use of observers to code what they observe. He referred in particular to an example that von Davier had offered of coding every interaction in a basketball game. With a planned missing data design, he said, "you can randomly assign who looks at which frame of the basketball game, and then, with the right kind of overlap, you can collect the kind of data you want in a much more efficient way, and not have all of that extra time and energy being spent trying to get everybody to watch every interaction and code every interaction."

Finally, Little suggested that planned missing data designs could be used to collect data more efficiently in the large batteries of tests used to assess personnel. Such intensive tests lead to fatigue and other factors that undermine their validity, he said, and the problem could be avoided, or at least ameliorated, with a planned missing data assessment protocol. "From that perspective, these [missing data] designs are the more valid, ethical way to go."

accurately requires being able to code a number of different aspects about what teams do, and that is difficult, Chao acknowledged.

Chao commented that a similar challenge faces the Army. "We [the Army] have platoons that go out. They do everything correctly, and yet the mission fails. What do we do to try to make that not happen again? It speaks to the criterion problem and how complex it is going to be in terms of looking at multiple levels of issues to consider."

Gerald Goodwin, of the U.S. Army Research Institute for the Behavioral and Social Sciences, emphasized that to really know whether a particular decision is good or bad, it is necessary to see that decision in the context of an overall strategy. As is the case with chess, it can be difficult to tell whether a move is good or bad without knowing how it fits with other moves in following an overall strategy. "It is not as simple as a correct or incorrect [move] or good or bad [move]. It could be any number of things. It is an indicator of a deeper sequence of performance that you are trying to capture, which is representing some level of skill that is the latent aspect that you are actually trying to estimate."

REFERENCES

Davison, M.L., and E.C. Davenport, Jr. (2002). Identifying criterion-related patterns of predictor scores using multiple regression. *Psychological Methods*, 7(4):468-484.

DeYoung, C.G., L.C. Quilty, and J.B. Peterson. (2007). Between facets and domains: 10 aspects of the Big Five. *Journal of Personality and Social Psychology*, 93(5):880-896.

Dudley, N.M., K.A. Orvis, J.E. Lebiecki, and J.M. Cortina. (2006). A meta-analytic investigation of conscientiousness in the prediction of job performance: Examining the intercorrelations and the incremental validity of narrow traits. *Journal of Applied Psychology*, 91(1):40-57.

Enders, C.K. (2010). *Applied Missing Data Analysis*. New York: Guilford Press.

Fan, J., D. Gao, S.A. Carroll, F.J. Lopez, T.S. Tian, and H. Meng. (2012). Testing the efficacy of a new procedure for reducing faking on personality tests within selection contexts. *Journal of Applied Psychology*, 97(4):866-880.

Graham, J.W. (2012). *Missing Data: Analysis and Design*. New York: Springer.

Halpin, P.F., and P. De Boeck. (2013). Modelling dyadic interaction with Hawkes processes. *Psychometrika* DOI: 10.1007/S11336-013-9329-1. Published online only. Available: http://link.springer.com/article/10.1007%2Fs11336-013-9329-1#page-1 [August 2013].

Landers, R.N., P.R. Sackett, and K.A. Tuzinski. (2011). Retesting after initial failure, coaching rumors, and warnings against faking in online personality measures for selection. *Journal of Applied Psychology*, 96(1):202-210.

Lievens, F., T. Buyse, and P.R. Sackett. (2005). The operational validity of a video-based situational judgment test for medical school admissions: Illustrating the importance of matching predictor and criterion construct domains. *Journal of Applied Psychology*, 90(3):442-452.

McHenry, J.J., L.M. Hough, J.L. Toquam, M.A. Hanson, and S. Ashworth. (1990). Project A validity results: The relationship between predictor and criterion domains. *Personnel Psychology*, 43(2):335-354.

Pulakos, E.D., S. Arad, M.A. Donovan, and K.E. Plamondon. (2000). Adaptability in the workplace: Development of a taxonomy of adaptive performance. *Journal of Applied Psychology,* 85(4):612-624.

Sackett, P.R., and F. Lievens. (2008). Personnel selection. In S.T. Fiske, A.E. Kazdin, and D.L. Schacter (Eds.), *Annual Review of Psychology* (vol. 10, pp. 419-450). Palo Alto, CA: Annual Reviews.

Sackett, P.R., M.L. Gruys, and J.E. Ellingson. (1998). Ability-personality interactions when predicting job performance. *Journal of Applied Psychology,* 83(4):545-556.

Shaffer, J.A., and B.E. Postlethwaite. (2012). A matter of context: A meta-analytic investigation of the relative validity of contextualized and noncontextualized personality measures. *Personnel Psychology,* 65(3):445-493.

Shen, W., and P.R. Sackett. (2010). *Predictive Power of Personality: Profile vs. Level Effects Predicting Extra-Role Performance.* Presented at the Society for Industrial and Organizational Psychology Conference, April, Atlanta, GA.

Shen, W., and P.R. Sackett. (2012). *The Relationship of Big Five Personality Profiles to Job Performance.* Presented at the Society for Industrial and Organizational Psychology Conference, April, San Diego, CA.

van Buuren, S. (2012). *Flexible Imputation of Missing Data.* Boca Raton, FL: CRC Press.

von Davier, A.A. and P.F. Halpin. (in press). *Collaborative Problem Solving and the Assessment of Cognitive Skills: Psychometric Considerations.* Princeton, NJ: Educational Testing Service. Upon publication, available: http://search.ets.org/researcher [August 2013].

6

Ethical Issues Related to Personnel Assessment and Selection

Because educational and pre-employment assessments can have a tremendous effect—for better or worse—on people's lives, a number of ethical issues may arise when designing, carrying out, and making decisions based on such assessments. Thus, in a departure from the workshop's other presentations, which were concerned mainly with the scientific and technical issues related to assessment, Rodney Lowman, a distinguished professor of psychology in the California School of Professional Psychology at Alliant International University in San Diego, devoted his presentation to potential ethical issues related to personnel assessment and selection. His intention, he said, was not to resolve the issues but rather to bring the questions to the attention of the workshop participants for present consideration and future contemplation.

A CASE STUDY OF THE FUTURE

Perhaps the best way to learn about ethics, Lowman said, is to examine thought-provoking case studies. He began his presentation by offering a detailed, albeit fictitious, case study that raised a number of potential ethical issues related to personnel assessment, selection, and assignment. Lowman gave the following fictitious account of a future scenario:

> The year is 2035. The recruiting function, now affectionately known as "HR Drone" has electronically scanned the social media accounts of all persons in the Army's target age range and integrated the results of those fitting the desired profile with high school and college tran-

> scripts of those who submitted their credentials to the Uniform Job Bank (almost all high school and college students did so, since most prospective employers required that). The Uniform Job Bank also contains the test results "voluntarily submitted" of all standardized academic tests taken throughout the academic career. A personalized invitation to apply for advanced assessment is [delivered] to the most promising of the candidates. [Thumb prints and iris eye scans proctor Internet-administered] interests-ability-personality tests and . . . a live team assessment simulation with other such candidates.
>
> A computer algorithm identifies the preferred profiles for a team position to be filled that is compatible with others already on the team. Diversity across genders and races is considered based on current underrepresented groups.
>
> . . . Once a year, Army personnel re-take interests-ability-personality tests as well as measures of proficiency and continued fitness for duty. . . . The results of brain scans, now effortlessly made at personal computers with an inexpensive BioCap are integrated into the database. . . . Personnel interests-ability-personality profiles are constantly scanned when team vacancies arise. Individuals learn of their matched team options and may apply for such vacancies on nomination.

While the reaction to this scenario from other workshop participants was mixed regarding the feasibility of such a future, Lowman's point was that many of these futuristic tools and technologies are not impossible to imagine, given current and emerging capabilities. And if those creating the tools and technologies do not anticipate and prepare for the ethical issues that will arise, Lowman cautioned that the practical utility of many tools may be limited.

CODES OF ETHICS

With the case study providing context for the challenges ahead, Lowman encouraged the workshop participants to examine some of the issues that it raised. "What ethical issues arise from this hypothetical scenario? How would we address those concerns?"

To answer these questions, he said, the first question is whose ethics should be used to address and resolve ethical issues and concerns? A variety of professions have ethics codes, he noted, and they are generally distinct.

One of the best-known codes of ethics is that of medicine, which dates back to the Hippocratic Oath from the fifth century BCE. In his oath Hippocrates addressed a number of areas still of concern to medical doctors today: competence ("I will apply [prescriptive] measures for the benefit of the sick, according to my ability and judgment"), avoiding conflicts of interest ("Whatever houses I may visit, I will come for the benefit of the sick, remaining free of all intentional injustice, of all mischief, and, in particular, of sexual relations with both female and male persons, be they free or slaves"), and avoiding doing harm to the patient ("I will keep them from harm and injustice") (Edelstein, 1943).

Psychologists have their own well-developed codes of ethics, Lowman said, which are of particular interest when discussing testing and assessments because primarily psychologists and those in related fields create the tests and they sometimes, but not always, oversee or influence how the tests are administered and interpreted. He chose to focus on the code of ethics of the American Psychological Association (APA), which was developed in 1953, making it one of the original codes of ethics for psychologists. It has been widely emulated around the world, he said, and it is more advanced than many others in how it thinks through areas of conflict.

The APA code of ethics, Lowman continued, "has 5 aspirational principles, which are things that people are supposed to think about and aspire to, and 10 enforceable standards." As an example of an aspirational principle, he exhibited the following principle, which concerns beneficence and nonmalevolence:

> Psychologists strive to benefit those with whom they work and take care to do no harm. In their professional actions, psychologists seek to safeguard the welfare and rights of those with whom they interact professionally and other affected persons, and the welfare of animal subjects of research. When conflicts occur among psychologists' obligations or concerns, they attempt to resolve these conflicts in a responsible fashion that avoids or minimizes harm. Because psychologists' scientific and professional judgments and actions may affect the lives of others, they are alert to and guard against personal, financial, social, organizational, or political factors that might lead to misuse of their influence. Psychologists strive to be aware of the possible effect of their own physical and mental health on their ability to help those with whom they work. (American Psychological Association, 2010)

Lowman also provided examples of the enforceable standards from the APA code of ethics. For example, Standard 2.04 says, "Psychologists' work is based upon established scientific and professional knowledge of the discipline." Standard 9.02, which has several parts related to assessments, says in part (a), "Psychologists administer, adapt, score, interpret or use assessment techniques, interviews, tests or instruments in a manner and for purposes that are appropriate in light of the research on or evidence of the usefulness and proper application of the techniques" (American Psychological Association, 2010).

"If you scan the psychology ethics codes of professional psychology organizations around the world," Lowman said, "you will find that most of them are saying some version of the same thing." That is, they tend to follow much the same lines as the APA code of ethics. Some of the common concerns are obtaining informed consent, avoiding harm, protecting the rights of participants in research, making sure that practice is based in scientifically obtained knowledge, avoiding multiple relationships that can harm others, and respecting the rights of the individuals with whom the psychologist works.

Most other professions have codes of ethics as well, Lowman said. Accountants, dentists, lawyers, social workers, nurses, and teachers—all of these have codes of ethics that define some version of what is appropriate behavior. One glaring exception is managers. "I would be happy to be proven wrong," Lowman said, "but there is no widely accepted code of ethics that managers are expected to follow." There has been a great deal of work aimed at professionalizing management, but there is as yet no recognized code of ethics for the profession. Lowman described a code of ethics that a group of students has created for managers—specifically, an "M.B.A. oath"—but he said that nothing of the sort has been adopted.

"This is a problem," he said. "It is a problem because we as psychologists and others who do this kind of work are the ones who often create the instruments, but it is managers who are the ones who use them to make decisions about what assessments, if any, to use." The psychologists and others who create the tests often have no real control over testing decisions. And in the absence of managerial ethics codes, decisions often end up being made not by scientific judgment but through laws and court rulings, which generally result in decisions that are slow and difficult to change. As an example he mentioned the Uniform Guidelines on Employee Selection Procedures of 1978, which have been "stuck in time" with less and less applicability but no political will to change them (U.S. Government, 1978). He noted that a recent article argued that the Uniform Guidelines have been a "detriment to the field of personnel selection" (McDaniel et al., 2011).

ETHICAL ISSUES RELATED TO EMERGING ASSESSMENT TECHNOLOGIES

To close, Lowman raised six specific ethical issues relevant to assessment technologies, and he discussed each briefly. His goals, he said, were to raise questions, not to answer them, and to trigger thought and discussion about the issues.

Issue 1. What are the ethical issues in expanding what is assessed from single variables or domains to profiles?

Lowman described an assessment of eight candidates for the position of city manager in a major U.S. city (Lowman, 1991). All the candidates were either already city managers or had an equally appropriate background. To help distinguish among them, personality profiles were created for each by assigning scores for six characteristics—enterprising, social, conventional, investigative, artistic, and realistic—and ranking those characteristics for each candidate. The average interest profile of the eight candidates combined had "enterprising," "social," and "conventional" as the three most prominent characteristics, "which is where you would expect a managerial profile to be," Lowman noted. But only one of the eight candidates matched this profile as an individual. By analyzing the candidates in this way, he said, it was possible to gain insight into their overall patterns of characteristics, which would not have been obvious looking at just their individual characteristics in isolation.

But such an approach raises certain ethical questions, Lowman said. If validity is an ethical obligation, what are the appropriate paradigms for validating inferences from profiles versus individual variables? Second, to what extent can some characteristics that may be relatively low in a profile, such as cognitive (or general) intelligence, be compensated for by other variables, such as emotional intelligence or team skills? And third, who decides issues related to profile fit? How should technical experts in assessment deal with others who have influence in making selection decisions?

Issue 2. Is it ethically more appropriate to administer tests "once and done" or on multiple occasions over a career?

Since it is becoming increasingly technically feasible to assess people frequently, Lowman asked, to what extent should that be done? Is it more fair or ethically appropriate to test on a "once and done" basis or to test on multiple occasions throughout a career, particularly as job requirements change? And what kinds of assessment and ethical issues arise if abilities or aptitudes, to take one example, are known to decline over time?

Issue 3. What are the ethical issues in selecting for "team fit" versus selecting the "best qualified" individual?

Concerning the selection of individuals based on team fit, Lowman raised several ethical issues: Is it ethically appropriate to evaluate people for real-life, high-risk decisions in the context of their fit with other people, such as the goodness of fit for teams? In particular, since the goodness of fit for a team presumably changes, based on the make-up of a team and the purposes for which the team was assembled, can that be a fair basis for selection? Furthermore, is it fair or ethical to make selections based on qualities over which an individual has no control? Finally, in assessing for "team fit," are the major criteria relatively stable and unchanging characteristics of people, such as personality dimensions, or are they potentially trainable behavioral skills that can be learned to some degree, and, ethically, does it matter?

Issue 4. Is it ethically appropriate to use biological assessments or molecular markers in assessment?

Do biological assessments and markers cross some sort of line—at the very least a perceptual line—that should not be crossed? Lowman said that he had recently shared the futuristic scenario he presented with a graduate class, and the only aspect of the scenario that bothered them was the use of biological and genetic type markers. Is there a substantive issue here, or just a perceptual one, and what difference does it make?

What should be the ethical "rules of engagement" for using biological molecular data in personnel selection? The science may not be quite there yet, but it is coming, Lowman predicted.

Finally, are these biological and genetic data sources really different in kind, conceptually and ethically, from cognitive ability, personality tests, and other psychological measures, or are they just something with which people are not yet familiar?

Later in the workshop, Gerald Goodwin, of the U.S. Army Research Institute for the Behavioral and Social Sciences, noted that the ethics of genetic information in military selection is not a concern for the foreseeable future. "Congress passed a law banning all organizations, federal and nonfederal," he explained, "from receiving, using, or retaining genetic information for . . . employment-related decisions." While there are exceptions to the law, including an exemption for the Department of Defense, "the Department of Defense has not opted to pursue it." Goodwin continued, "regardless of the ethics of the matter, it is illegal, and it is illegal for everyone, pretty much" (see U.S. Government, 2008).

Issue 5. What feedback are candidates entitled to receive?

Is feedback on assessment results an ethical right? The issue can be thought of in analogy with credit ratings, Lowman said. "You can find out what your credit ratings were. You still get turned down, but at least you know what some of the data were."

According to the APA ethics code, in most types of testing it is required that anyone who is tested should receive feedback. However, one exception is in the case of testing done for the purpose of personnel selection.

"I am not sure that was a good ethical change to have made in the code," he said, "but that is what it is."

In addition, which information—if any—should be withheld if feedback is given? And what sorts of issues arise concerning feedback on biological and molecular results?

Issue 6. What are the ethics of using unproctored or proctored Internet testing?

If all testing will ultimately be able to be conducted online, what ethical issues arise concerning the need to ensure validity and protect applicants? As more and more organizations are moving to unproctored Internet testing because it is more efficient and less expensive, is additional proctored assessment needed? And is online assessment of groups and teams ethically fair and appropriate?

Lowman ended with three quotations intended to provoke further thought. He cited former Supreme Court Justice Potter Stewart as having said: "Ethics is knowing the difference between what you have a right to do and what is right to do." And from philosopher Bertrand Russell: "An ethical person ought to do more than he's required to do and less than he's allowed to do." And from Lowman himself: "Ethical questions and conflicts anticipated and discussed tend to be ethical issues avoided."

REFERENCES

American Psychological Association. (2010). *Ethical Principles of Psychologists and Code of Conduct. With the 2010 Amendments.* Washington, DC: American Psychological Association. Available: http://www.apa.org/ethics/code/principles.pdf [July 2013].

Edelstein, L. (1943). *The Hippocratic Oath: Text, Translation, and Interpretation*. Baltimore, MD: Johns Hopkins University Press.

Lowman, R.L. (1991). *The Clinical Practice of Career Assessment: Interests, Abilities, and Personality.* Washington, DC: American Psychological Association.

McDaniel, M.A., S. Kepes, and G.C. Banks. (2011). The Uniform Guidelines are a detriment to the field of personnel selection. *Industrial and Organizational Psychology,* 4(4):494-514.

U.S. Government. (1978). Uniform Guidelines on Employee Selection Procedures. Part 1607, Title 29, Labor, Subtitle B–Regulation Relating to Labor, Chapter XIV–Equal Employment Opportunity Commission. Available: http://www.gpo.gov/fdsys/pkg/CFR-2011-title29-vol4/xml/CFR-2011-title29-vol4-part1607.xml [July 2013].

U.S. Government. (2008). The Genetic Information Nondiscrimination Act of 2008. Equal Employment Opportunity Commission. Available: http://www.eeoc.gov/laws/statutes/gina.cfm [July 2013].

7

A Way Forward

During the workshop's second day, Earl Hunt, an emeritus professor of psychology at the University of Washington in Seattle, presented "Assessing Cognitive Skills: Case History, Diagnosis, and Treatment Plan." Although his focus was specifically on cognitive skills, rather than the broader range of traits of interest to the military, his talk captured a number of possible ways forward, as the Army seeks to improve its assessment and selection processes. He offered a useful way of thinking about the constraints and the challenges in that endeavor. Although Hunt's presentation occurred in the second day's panel on individual differences and predicting individual behavior, it has general relevance to how the Army might proceed to take the next leap forward in assessments, in light of the information shared at the workshop.

THE BORING BOX

When the French psychologist Alfred Binet developed the first broadly usable intelligence test in the early 1900s, Hunt said, what he really discovered was "drop in from the sky" testing. "He found that you can drop in from the sky and, out of context, ask a bunch of questions of somebody and get a reasonable—not perfect, but a reasonable—idea of their cognitive skills with very little cost." Hunt attributed the phrase "drop in from the sky" to Robert Mislevy of the Educational Testing Service and the University of Maryland, College Park.

Binet's "drop in from the sky" tests, Hunt continued, could be done in a limited time period, and they reasonably assessed a significant portion, but not all, of an individual's cognitive skills. A century of testing has refined Binet's paradigm, he said, but it has not expanded the range of skills tapped by Binet's test in any major way.

Hunt said that this testing approach, while very valuable, is limited by a conceptual problem that is inherent in the approach. In 1923, the psychologist Edwin Boring defined "intelligence" as "what the tests test," which were those cognitive skills that could fit into the box of time allowed for the "drop in from the sky" testing, and thus, Hunt observed, came the term, "Boring's box." Although most psychologists will demur that this is not what they mean by "intelligence," in practice this is exactly how it has been defined. A century of work has produced useful cognitive models for the skills that the tests evaluate—but those are only the behaviors that *fit in the box*, he emphasized.

As an aside, Hunt noted that Binet's test was still a valuable achievement because there is a great deal of overlap between the cognitive skills required for life and the cognitive skills evaluated by the test. "It's not perfect, but there is enough overlap that this information is quite useful."

With respect to the current status of testing, Hunt said that tests for behaviors and attributes fit into Boring's box, and almost a century of competent research has made these tests very good—within the limits of the box. He cited as an example the Armed Services Vocational Aptitude Battery (ASVAB), saying it is the distant heir to the Army Alpha test, which was created almost 100 years ago. The developers of ASVAB "have been competent people," Hunt said. "They have known what they're doing, and it is arrogant to consider that you are so much smarter than the people who went before, that you are going to make a great improvement."

Bending the Box

According to Hunt, there are ways to bend Boring's box a little to fit a few more things into it. The development of computer testing, he said, was one such example, as was adaptive testing and item response theory. To understand ways in which cognitive testing may be improved in the future, one can look for other ways to bend the box.

Perhaps the biggest way, he suggested, is to use new constructs of the types that were discussed in the workshop presentations by Michael Kane and Christopher Patrick (see Chapter 3). In particular, he pointed to working memory capacity and the ability to focus and control attention as offering very promising ways to bend the box. The relevant tests include dichotic stimulus paradigms, which stress the control of attention; N-back tests, which stress short-term memory functioning; and Stroop-like tests, which require a resolution of conflict between signals.

A second type of box bender is the dual cognition task. "For a long time," Hunt said, "people have talked about two cognitive systems": the fast gut response and the slower, more thoughtful response. The psychologist Jonathan Haidt (2006) has used the analogy of an elephant and its rider to describe how these two systems interact. The job of the rider, Hunt recounted, is to keep the elephant on task, but while the rider is rational and develops plans for how things should be done, the elephant is "pretty stupid." For example, the elephant operates according to statistical associations in the environment. "The elephant says that crime is going up because you get a lot of reports on TV. It's the rider who says, 'No, crime is going down. Look at the statistics.'" The elephant is also prone to emotional reactions.

And what happens, Hunt continued, is that the elephant biases the rider. When conscious thought—the rider—comes up with various possible solutions to a cognitive task, the elephant can bias the rider to choosing one solution over the other (Kahneman, 2011).

Hunt discussed two particular areas where managing the elephant is important, and these, he suggested, offer the possibility for tests that bend the box. One of the areas is overcoming decision biases. Today, there is a very large body of literature on decisions and decision biases which is largely not reflected in current cognitive testing, Hunt said. A well-known example is the "Linda problem," which requires a person to overcome the normal tendency to apply a representativeness heuristic to solving a problem (Tversky and Kahneman, 1982).

The second area is overcoming unconscious social biases. *Blindspot*, a recent book by Mahzarin Banaji and Tony Greenwald (2013), offers a number of examples of social situations in which bias affects the way people deal with other people. Racial prejudice is the obvious example, Hunt said. "People who don't consider themselves racist, who will not endorse racist attitudes publicly, can be shown to have what's best described as an elephant-style response to members of other races, and that will influence their behavior, although they are not aware of it."

Hunt suggested two other ways of bending the box. One is to work with orientation skills. There are a number of jobs in which orientation skills are important, such as maintenance on Navy ships where people must work in confined spaces surrounded by live wires. Orientation skills are also important in firing artillery and in a number of other tasks. They can be evaluated using virtual environment techniques (Allahyar and Hunt, 2003).

The other approach is to measure processing speed, which has been claimed to be a very important factor in intelligence (Jensen, 2006). The idea is that simple reaction times can reveal something about the state of a person's nervous system. However, Hunt said that he is very suspicious of this data. "I think that if you do the experiments the way they did, you will get the results they did, but there are some aspects [open to] interpretation, and also it is an open question whether this is a significant source of variation in young adult populations."

In all of these efforts to bend the box and squeeze more in, a number of constraints must be kept in mind, Hunt said. First, the Boring box is full, so if something new goes in, something old must come out. The issue is not the bivariate correlation; it is the incremental validity (will the new method increase the predictive ability of an existing method of assessment?). Furthermore, many of these new methods, especially the working memory methods, are time hogs. They require time to familiarize the people taking the test with the equipment or the procedure.

A second issue is that the nature of some of these new tasks can actually change with practice. "This is why I'm suspicious of the reaction time data," Hunt said, "because they allow very little time for practice. The result is that the factor structure of a reaction time task, including the working memory task, may change over practice and over days." Hunt mentioned research studied by Bittner and colleagues (1986) that found that, while the within-day reliability of the tasks they were measuring was very high, the across-day reliability was not as high. "That doesn't mean they're invalid," he said, "but it means that it would be harder to fit them into Boring's box."

Breaking the Box

The other approach to improving the measurement of cognitive skills significantly would be to move outside Boring's box, Hunt said. There are certain abilities "that we have to find a way to evaluate if we are going to increase predictivity on the basis of cognition," he said, adding that evaluating those abilities will almost certainly require breaking the box.

One example Hunt gave is people's ability to take multiple perspectives—to not just jump to a conclusion but to realize that the problem can look very different when considered from different angles. This is important in a variety of areas. One is trouble-shooting mechanical problems. Another is dealing with social problems, which have been a particular problem when members of the military come in contact with indigenous populations, Hunt said. "You don't necessarily have to agree with another person's perspective on the problem, but you'd better know it."

Another example of breaking the box is studying performance in groups and teams, as presented during this workshop by Tannenbaum,

Woolley, and DeChurch (see Chapter 4). As an aside, Hunt noted that he distinguishes between a group and a team when characterizing performance. Much of the academic research is done on groups, meaning collections of people who have not met previously but who are assembled for the purpose of the research. Sometimes researchers will even have leadership studies in which they bring a group of people together who do not know each other and assign one of them to be the "leader."

"That's not the way the drill sergeant works," Hunt said. "Military teams exist over time. Privates do not lead teams, but they can disrupt them. So the Army has a real need to be able to predict a person's performance in a team."

A third way to break the box would be to study how well people are able to organize and carry out plans. "Basically this is the ability to get up, organize yourself, order goals, often delay gratification," he explained. The ability to delay gratification has been shown to be particularly important—its degree in children in preschool can predict performance on the Scholastic Aptitude Test (SAT) 10 to 12 years later (Duckworth et al., 2010). Setting goals and then meeting them is also a critically important trait.

"These skills can be measured," Hunt said, "but not inside the box. I can't think of any way to measure these cognitive skills within Boring's box."

How might they be measured? Hunt noted that relevant information is already physically obtainable in people's electronic footprints: school records, credit transactions, Facebook friends, court records, and so on. Should these things be used? To that question, Hunt said there are various ethical and legal issues to consider, but it might be possible to get informed consent under certain situations.

Another approach would be to monitor recruit training carefully, including selected situational tests. This would provide a great deal of information and could probably improve classification, but it would also increase the expense of recruit training.

"So here's my take-home message," Hunt said, "Boring's box has been cleaned out." He offered an analogy with mining gold in California. "It was a very good idea in 1849. I point out that the only real fortune that came out of it was Levi Straus, and what he did was make miners' trousers. . . . He took a different perspective on the problem and remembered that the goal was to get rich, not to mine gold."

Hunt predicted it will continue to be possible to make minor improvements by further research inside the box or by bending the box. But major advancements in assessment, he concluded in his written notes provided to all workshop attendees, "will have to move out of Boring's box, to examine cognitive talents that simply cannot be revealed in a two or three hour testing session. Any such movement will be costly. However, something can be costly and still be cost-effective. The military cannot make the best use of recruits' talents unless those talents are known."

FINAL THOUGHTS

As the workshop's final speaker, committee member Randall Engle revisited the major points of the invited presentations and offered his thoughts on emerging themes and the future of measuring human capabilities. Throughout his summary, Engle repeatedly reminded the workshop participants of the study sponsor's perspective, as presented by Gerald Goodwin, of the U.S. Army Research Institute for the Behavioral and Social Sciences, who had noted that the statement of task for the larger study calls for the committee to make recommendations on basic research. Engle said he was thrilled to see this call for recommendations on basic research because the field seems to him to need fresh thinking about important concepts such as working memory, rather than just redoing the same constructs over and over again. Working memory, he explained, is actually many things, and if researchers just stop at measuring the same constructs that have been assumed to capture it, because they know how to make those measurements, then the field has basically died. By undertaking research at a more fundamental level, as Engle understands basic research, new ways of thinking about concepts such as working memory can emerge and move the field forward. And he believes that kind of research is important.

Engle also identified a recurring theme across many of the presentations: the emergence of an electronic and technological revolution in the way we communicate with each other. "Web-based testing is going to happen," he predicted. "I think there are really exciting things about that, and some real dangerous things about it—dangerous in a very broad sense." And while the workshop discussions had not delved deeply into those dangerous issues, he continued, Rodney Lowman's presentation on ethics provided the participants with difficult questions to think about as modes and methods of assessments move forward. Engle also noted that Paul Sackett's discussion of real-time faking in testing (see Chapter 5) presents significantly new implications for Web-based testing. Engle also validated Sackett's concerns by describing his own research, which suggests working memory tests performed online using verbal measures are more susceptible to faking than spatial tasks because test-takers will write down the verbal cues rather than retaining them in memory. "Many people are just going to Web-based things" Engle said, "without really looking at the consequences, costs, and benefits of doing that. And I think that's a really, really important issue to think about here. The faking, I think, is all part and parcel of that."

Over the course of the workshop, Engle also noted a relationship between testing knowledge and learning. Fred Oswald (see Chapter 2) spoke extensively about declarative knowledge, but "he didn't say anything about how one gets that declarative knowledge." Engle noted that he found it curious that the idea of learning did not receive much attention during the workshop except in relation to group composition, especially during the final panel presentations (see Chapter 4). The workshop's keynote speaker, Alina von Davier, also emphasized that valid assessments should reflect that people learn and use skills in collaborative ways (see Chapter 5). Cognitive abilities, Engle said, are important because they relate to learning, and the ability to learn, to acquire a lot of information appropriate to a situation quickly, is important to performance and improving performance. But learning had not been talked about much at the workshop, he observed.

In speaking about the utility of noncognitive skills in performance predictions, Engle indicated his understanding that (at least some time ago) research in personality factors demonstrated "almost no relationship between the noncognitive measures and task performance." "They just were not very predictive," he said. He then related a personal story about a meeting with Navy personnel, during which he inquired, "So why would the Navy keep using these noncognitive measures?" The answer he received captured much of the spirit of this workshop: "It's because they predict attrition very well, and for every one percent of attrition that we can reduce in the Navy, we're saving the American public about $10 million." Engle recalled his reaction, "Okay, well, that's an important one percent." He continued, "So I think thinking about all of the variety of ways that these different assessments can become important is a big deal."

Engle also noted an emerging theme of creating valid tests for administration across the population, especially concerning tests of personality. He noted that very different models may be required to understand both cognitive and noncognitive attributes of different groups. "These things are much more complicated than we would ever like to believe," Engle admitted.

In the workshop's final moments, committee chair Jack Stuster reiterated the challenge of predicting performance through conventional testing: "Tests are clearly analogs for the actual observed behaviors that you would prefer to have to inform your selection decisions. But practical issues greatly constrain the fidelity and, as a consequence, the validity of those predictions." While admitting that practical issues may place certain constraints on the way forward, Engle concluded his summary with an encouraging word. Recalling Earl Hunt's earlier presentation on Boring's box, Engle said, "Most of the tests we have are inside that box, and it seems to me that a big part of what this workshop is about is sort of erasing the lines of that box and finding out, 'Are there better ways that we can do these things?' And I think there are."

REFERENCES

Allahyar, M., and E. Hunt. (2003). The assessment of spatial orientation using virtual reality techniques. *International Journal of Testing,* 3(3):263-275.

Banaji, M., and A.G. Greenwald. (2013). *Blindspot: Hidden Biases of Good People.* New York: Delacorte.

Bittner, A.C., R.C. Carter, R.S. Kennedy, M.M. Harbeson, and M. Krause. (1986). Performance evaluation tests for environmental research (PETER): Evaluation of 114 measures. *Perceptual and Motor Skills,* 63(2):683-708.

Duckworth, A.L., E. Tsukayama, and H. May. (2010). Establishing causality using longitudinal hierarchical linear modeling: An illustration predicting achievement from self-control. *Social Psychological and Personality Science,* 1(4):311-317.

Haidt, J. (2006). *The Happiness Hypothesis: Finding Modern Truth in Ancient Wisdom.* New York: Basic Books.

Jensen, A.R. (2006). *Clocking the Mind: Mental Chronometry and Individual Differences.* Amsterdam, The Netherlands: Elsevier.

Kahneman, D. (2011). *Thinking, Fast and Slow.* New York: Farrar, Strauss, and Giroux.

Tversky, A., and D. Kahneman. (1982). Judgments of and by representativeness. In D. Kahneman, P. Slovic, and A. Tversky (Eds.), *Judgment Under Uncertainty: Heuristics and Biases* (pp. 84-100). Cambridge, UK: Cambridge University Press.

Appendix

Workshop Agenda and Participants

AGENDA

Workshop on New Directions in Assessing Individuals and Groups
April 3-4, 2013

Workshop Goals

1. Facilitate interdisciplinary dialogue on the current and future state-of-the-science in measurement of individual capabilities and the combination of individual capabilities to create collective capacity to perform.
2. Inform the design of a maximally effective selection and assignment system.

Wednesday, April 3

8:00 am **Workshop Check-In**

9:00 **Welcome from the National Research Council**
Robert M. Hauser, Executive Director, Division of Behavioral and Social Sciences and Education

Overview of the Board on Behavioral, Cognitive, and Sensory Sciences
Barbara A. Wanchisen, Director, Board on Behavioral, Cognitive, and Sensory Sciences

Introductions

9:30 **Workshop Objectives and Study Overview**
Jack Stuster, Anacapa Sciences, Inc., and Chair, Committee on Measuring Human Capabilities

10:00 **Sponsor's Perspective**
Gerald (Jay) Goodwin, Chief, Foundational Science, U.S. Army Research Institute for the Behavioral and Social Sciences

10:45 **Break**

11:00 **Setting the Stage: The Evolving Goals of Candidate Testing and Its Role in Personnel Selection**
Fred Oswald, Rice University

12:00 pm **Keynote Address: Psychometrics for a New Generation of Assessments**
Alina von Davier, Research Director, Center for Advanced Psychometrics, Educational Testing Service

12:30 **Working Lunch**
Jack Stuster, Chair
Topic: Discussion of ideas presented in Keynote Address

1:15 **Emerging Constructs and Theory**
Part One: Invited Presentations
A Psychoneurometric Approach to Individual Differences Assessment
Christopher Patrick, Florida State University
The Emerging Cognitive Constructs of Working Memory Capacity and Executive Attention
Michael Kane, University of North Carolina at Greensboro
The Agentic Self: Action-Control Beliefs
Todd Little, Kansas University

Part Two: Roundtable Discussion with Committee Members and Invited Presenters

3:30 **Break**

3:45 **Ethical Implications of Future Testing Techniques and Personnel Selection Paradigms**
Rodney Lowman, Alliant International University

Reactions from Committee Members

4:45 **Conclude Day One**

Thursday, April 4

8:30 am **Day Two Workshop Check-In Open**

9:00 **Summary of Day One and Overview of Day Two**
Jack Stuster, Anacapa Sciences, Inc., and Chair, Committee on Measuring Human Capabilities

9:15 **Measuring Individual Differences and Predicting Individual Performance**
Part One: Invited Presentations
Taxonomic Structure for Thinking About Ways to Improve the Quality of Selection Systems
Paul Sackett, University of Minnesota
Rethinking Interests
James Rounds, University of Illinois at Urbana-Champaign
Assessing Cognitive Skills: Case History, Diagnosis, and Treatment Plan
Earl Hunt, University of Washington

10:15 **Break**

10:30 **Measuring Individual Differences and Predicting Individual Performance,** Continued
Part Two: Roundtable Discussion with Committee Members and Invited Presenters

12:00 pm **Working Lunch**
Jack Stuster, Chair
Topic: Continued roundtable discussion with committee members and invited presenters

12:45 **Group Composition Processes and Performance**
Part One: Invited Presentations
Team Composition: Theory, Practice, and the Future
Scott Tannenbaum, Group for Organizational Effectiveness
Understanding and Enabling the Collective Capabilities of Teams
Leslie DeChurch, Georgia Institute of Technology
Collective Intelligence in the Performance of Human Groups
Anita Williams Woolley, Carnegie Mellon University

Part Two: Roundtable Discussion with Committee Members and Invited Presenters

3:15 **Break**

3:30 **Cross-cutting Links and Research Gaps: Roundtable Discussion with Committee Members and All Invited Presenters**

4:00 **Workshop Implications**
Part One: Invited Presentation
Summary of Emerging Themes
Randall Engle, Georgia Institute of Technology, and Member, Committee on Measuring Human Capabilities

Part Two: Reactions from Invited Presenters and Committee Members

4:45 **Closing Comments**
Jack Stuster, Chair

5:00 **Adjourn**

PARTICIPANTS

Committee Members

Jack W. Stuster (*Chair*), Anacapa Sciences, Inc.
Georgia T. Chao, Michigan State University
Randall W. Engle, Georgia Institute of Technology
Leaetta Hough, Dunnette Group, Ltd.
Patrick C. Kyllonen, Educational Testing Service
John J. McArdle, University of Southern California
Stephen Stark, University of South Florida

Workshop Presenters and Panelists

Leslie DeChurch, Georgia Institute of Technology
Earl Hunt, University of Washington
Michael Kane, University of North Carolina at Greensboro
Todd Little, Kansas University
Rodney Lowman, Alliant International University
Fred Oswald, Rice University
Christopher Patrick, Florida State University
James Rounds, University of Illinois at Urbana-Champaign
Paul Sackett, University of Minnesota
Scott Tannenbaum, Group for Organizational Effectiveness
Alina von Davier, Educational Testing Service
Anita Williams Woolley, Carnegie Mellon University

Guests of the Sponsor (U.S. Army Research Institute for the Behavioral and Social Sciences, ARI)

Paul Gade, George Washington University and ARI (retired)
Gerald Goodwin, ARI
Tonia Heffner, ARI
Robert Kilcullen, ARI
Jennifer Klafehn, ARI
Kate LaPort, ARI
Peter Legree, ARI
Karin Orvis, ARI
Lynne Rochette, ARI
Andrew Slaughter, ARI

Members of the Board on Behavioral, Cognitive, and Sensory Sciences

Jennifer S. Cole, University of Illinois at Urbana-Champaign
Daniel R. Ilgen, Michigan State University
James S. Jackson, University of Michigan, Ann Arbor

National Research Council Staff

Shenae Bradley, Division on Engineering and Physical Sciences
Elizabeth Cady, National Academy of Engineering
Cherie Chauvin, Board on Behavioral, Cognitive, and Sensory Sciences
Jennifer Diamond, Board on Behavioral, Cognitive, and Sensory Sciences
Renée L. Wilson Gaines, Board on Behavioral, Cognitive, and Sensory Sciences
Robert M. Hauser, Division of Behavioral and Social Sciences and Education
Margaret Hilton, Board on Behavioral, Cognitive, and Sensory Sciences
Jatryce Jackson, Board on Behavioral, Cognitive, and Sensory Sciences
Ellen Kimmel, Information Services
Rebecca Morgan, Information Services
Daniel Talmage, Division on Engineering and Physical Sciences
Barbara A. Wanchisen, Board on Behavioral, Cognitive, and Sensory Sciences
Tina Winters, Board on Behavioral, Cognitive, and Sensory Sciences

Registered Attendees

In addition to those listed above, the following individuals registered to attend the public workshop either in person or virtually through the live webcast.

Neil Albert, Spencer Foundation
Zach Alessi-Friedlander, office of the Chief of Staff of the Army Strategic Studies Group
Terry Allard, Office of Naval Research
Jane Arabian, Office of the Under Secretary of Defense (Personnel and Readiness)
Zunair Ashfaq, University of Pennsylvania
Sujeeta Bhatt, U.S. Department of Defense
Kate Bleckley, Civil Aerospace Medical Institute, Federal Aviation Administration
John Bodnar, Office of the Director of National Intelligence
Sue Bogner, Institute for the Study of Human Error, LLC
Joshua Breslau, RAND Corporation

Cristina Byrne, Federal Aviation Administration
Kerri Chik, Aptima, Inc.
Angelo Collins, CENTRA Technology, Inc.
Nancy Cooke, Arizona State University
Jeffrey Cooper, National Security Sector SAIC
Mary Cummings, Massachusetts Institute of Technology
Cathie Currie, Altshuller Institute
David Desaulniers, U.S. Nuclear Regulatory Commission
Abigail Desjardins, NSI
David Dorsey, National Security Agency
Lauren Fairley-Wright, U.S. Department of Labor
Gonzalo Ferro, PDRI
Meredith Ferro, PDRI
Hannah Foldes, PDRI
Pamela Frugoli, U.S. Department of Labor Employment and Training Administration
Joe Funderburke, office of the Chief of Staff of the Army Strategic Studies Group
Hal Greenwald, MITRE
Kelly Hale, Design Interactive, Inc.
Kara Hall, National Cancer Institute
Amy Haufler, Johns Hopkins University Applied Physics Laboratory
Albert Holland, NASA Johnson Space Center
Valerie Holt, Lehigh University
Amy Holtz, BSI
Todd Horowitz, National Cancer Institute
Niav Hughes, U.S. Nuclear Regulatory Commission
Michael Ingerick, HumRRO
Kris Inman, National Intelligence University
Garth Jensen, OPNAV N9
Cheyanne Jones, Advocatee
James Kajdasz, National Intelligence University
Charles Keil, National Security Agency
Inki Kim, Pennsylvania State University
Deirdre Knapp, HumRRO
Tracy Laabs, Strategic Analysis, Inc.
Michael McDaniel, Virginia Commonwealth University
Jill McQuade, Assistant Secretary of Defense for Research and Engineering
Gerald J. Melican, The College Board
Julia Milton, Consortium of Social Science Associations
Amy Mistretta, National Institute on Aging
Wendy Nelson, National Cancer Institute

David Neri, Office of Naval Research
Cynthia Null, NASA Engineering and Safety Center
Janet Okamoto, Mayo Clinic
Mary Parker, Institute for Palliative and Hospice Training, Inc.
Misha Pavel, National Science Foundation
James Pepitone, Humaneering Institute
Linda Pierce, Federal Aviation Administration, Civil Aerospace Medical Institute
Robert Pool, Digital Pens, LLC
Gerald Powell, office of the Chief of Staff of the Army Strategic Studies Group
Jennifer Rasmussen, SHL
Krista Ratwani, Aptima, Inc.
Leslie Richards, University of the District of Columbia
Dylan Schmorrow, Assistant Secretary of Defense for Research and Engineering
Katharine Shobe, Office of Naval Research
John Skinner, Valtera Corporation
Amanda Snook, National Threat Assessment Center, U.S. Secret Service
Amber Sprenger, MITRE Corporation
Kay Stanney, Design Interactive, Inc.
Marc Steinberg, Office of Naval Research
William Strickland, HumRRO
John Tangney, Office of Naval Research
Catherine Tinsley, Georgetown University
Nancy Tippins, Valtera Corporation
Nick Vasilopoulos, National Security Agency
Alexander Walker, Aptima, Inc.
Susan Winter, University of Maryland
Michelle Wisecarver, PDRI
Mary Zalesny, office of the Chief of Staff of the Army Strategic Studies Group